History's Most Powerful Witches

Their Life, Witchcraft and Spells

Desmond Wilde

Copyrights

All rights reserved. © Desmond Wilde and Maplewood Publishing No part of this publication or the information in it may be quoted from or reproduced in any form by means such as printing, scanning, photocopying, or otherwise without prior written permission of the copyright holder.

Disclaimer and Terms of Use

Effort has been made to ensure that the information in this book is accurate and complete. However, the author and the publisher do not warrant the accuracy of the information, text, and graphics contained within the book due to the rapidly changing nature of science, research, known and unknown facts, and internet. The author and the publisher do not hold any responsibility for errors, omissions, or contrary interpretation of the subject matter herein. This book is presented solely for motivational and informational purposes only. The publisher and author of this book does not control or direct users' actions and are not responsible for the information or content shared, harm and/or action of the book readers. The presentation of the information is without contract or any type of guarantee assurance. This book is not meant to be used, nor should it be used, to diagnose or treat any medical condition. For diagnosis or treatment of any medical problem, consult your own physician. The publisher and author are not responsible for any specific health or allergy needs that may require medical supervision and are not liable for any damages or negative consequences from any treatment, action, application or preparation, to any person reading or following the information in this book. References, if any, are provided for informational purposes only and do not constitute endorsement of any websites or other sources. Readers should be aware that the websites listed in this book, if any, may change.

ISBN: 978-1530727186

Printed in the United States

Contents

Contents _____ 3
Introduction _____ 1
Medea _____ 3
   Medea's spell _____ 10
Agnes Sampson _____ 12
   Agnes' spell _____ 20
Alice Kyteler _____ 23
   Alice's spell _____ 30
Marie Laveau _____ 33
   Marie's spell _____ 40
Merga Bien _____ 43
   Merga's spell _____ 49
Agnes Waterhouse _____ 53
   Agnes's spell _____ 61
Malin Matsdotter _____ 65
   Malin's spell _____ 71
Mother Shipton _____ 73
   Mother Shipton's spell _____ 78
Joan Wytte _____ 81
   Joan's spell _____ 86
Rosaleen "Roie" Norton _____ 89
   Rosaleen's spell _____ 96
Conclusion _____ 99
Further Reading _____ 101

Image Credits_____103
More Books by Desmond Wilde_____105

Introduction

Witches have always worried, scared, and fascinated people in equal measure. From dark magic to home remedies, they have been part of the cultural landscape for people around the world. From Europe to the Americas, Asia to Africa, the idea of women who delve deep into magic has created some of the most enduring stories in the history of humanity. Often, these stories blend the real with the unreal, truth with fiction, and magic with the mundane. In this book, we will look at witches from across the world and across many thousands of years.

Witches are not always welcome. Often, they are feared. People worry about satanic practices and dark magic. Should a child fall sick, it is not uncommon for people to blame a local woman. Many have been falsely accused of witchcraft throughout history, and sometimes, these people have been killed as a result. Sometimes, even the rumored practice of dark magic can be enough to condemn a person to be burned at the stake.

Throughout this book, we will look into the history of witchcraft as it has been practiced by people over the ages. Not only that, but we will look into some of the spells that they relied upon for their power. By studying their specific arts, we can better understand the scope and the power of witchcraft. If you would like to know more about history's most powerful witches, then read on and discover some of the strangest, oddest, most magical, and most twisted tales in human history.

Medea

The further we travel back into the ancient world, the harder it becomes to discern myth from reality. In examining witches from Ancient Greece, this becomes even more difficult. Perhaps, then, it becomes more important to consider the legend. While the stories that have been passed down over the centuries are almost certainly more fiction than fact, they do provide us with a huge amount of information. For example, examining the most famous witches of Greek folklore gives us a keen indication of exactly how such magical practitioners were considered in Greek society and how other Greeks viewed these people purported to be witches. The legends tell us what powers normal people believed witches possessed, as well as their expectations as to how these spells might be used. Thanks in no small part to the fact that Greek culture has helped to shape modern western civilization in many, many ways, the legends we have about witches in Ancient Greece provide the foundation for much of our current views.

Of all the witches in Ancient Greek legends, perhaps the most famous (and the most powerful) is Medea. Supposedly the daughter of a king, the niece of another witch (Circe,) and even the granddaughter of a sun god, she is integral to the tale of Jason. Along with his band of Argonauts, Jason set about a quest to steal the Golden Fleece. An enchantress, a priestess, and – above all else – a practitioner of powerful magic, Medea was once the paramour of Jason, but as Euripides writes, was abandoned when Jason came across another woman. In the play named after her, Medea plots her revenge. One of the oldest stories passed down through the centuries, Euripides's Medea teaches us not only what the Ancient Greeks thought witches could do, but also how powerful they were in the Mediterranean during the Bronze Age.

The crux of the story between Jason and Medea begins after the former set out on his search for the Golden Fleece. According to legend, this item was the fleece taken from a golden-haired ram that roamed around the area of Colchis. The Golden Fleece was not just valuable, but was also an inherent indicator of one's right to rule. Through its possession, Jason would prove his rightful kingship. In the story, Medea met Jason and fell in love. Her father was the king in possession of the Golden Fleece. Despite his wariness of the newcomer who demanded his valuable treasure, he noted his daughter falling in love. In order to demonstrate the strength of her feelings, Medea resolved to help the hero in his quest. In return, she asked for Jason's hand in marriage. Impressed by the power of Medea and hoping to complete his quest, Jason agreed.

During the course of Jason's quest for the Golden Fleece, he had to prove his worthiness by completing a series of tasks. Set by Medea's father Aeëtes, Jason had to demonstrate his resolve and kingship through these tests. He relied on his magical cohort to complete them. The first of these involved having to plow a field. Rather than a normal piece of farming, however, he had to use fire-breathing oxen and set them in the yoke himself. To get around the fire-breathing viciousness of these beasts, Jason relied on Medea's skills as a witch. She supplied him with a special cream, which when rubbed on his skin, protected him against burning. Once under her protection, Jason was able to bend the oxen to his will and plow the field. This first task shows us the Greeks' belief in the healing and protective abilities of witches.

The second task is also related to farming. This time, Jason had to sow dragon's teeth into the same field. The task is a trick, however, as the sown teeth emerged out of the ground as skeleton soldiers to battle against Jason. But the hero was forewarned. Medea was aware of what would happen and warned her love of what to expect. She told Jason to throw a rock into the midst of the crowd. Confused, the skeletal warriors turned on one another, unware of who threw the rock. The skeletons began to fight with one another, leaving Jason free to complete the task, once more buoyed by the help of Medea the witch. This kind of awareness and understanding of the world is a skillset still attributed to witches around the world. A comprehension of nature and the supernatural is an essential part of witchcraft and is possessed only by those skilled in the magical arts. This, too, is a feature of witchcraft that continues through to the modern age.

The final task was the most difficult. To prove his worthiness, Jason had to steal the Golden Fleece from the tree where it is kept. Wrapped around the foot of the tree was a fearsome dragon who never slept. This watchful reptilian guard killed anyone who came too close. According to the instructions set by Aeëtes, Jason had to fight and kill this dragon. Only then would he be permitted to take the Fleece for himself. Once again, Jason turned to his paramour for help. Medea concocted a special potion, mixing together herbs and spices designed to put the dragon to sleep. Jason applied the potion, put the dragon to sleep, and stole away with the Golden Fleece. Along with Medea and his team of Argonauts, he sailed away. For anyone familiar with witchcraft, the idea of creating potions and salves is a familiar feature of magical practice. That they are powerful enough to lull a dragon to sleep speaks volumes about Medea's abilities as a witch.

But there's a darker side to the story. Once Medea and Jason complete their last task, Medea didn't leave her home quietly. In order to get away from her father, Aeëtes, Medea and Jason came up with a plan. Smitten by Jason, Medea murdered her brother in order to distract the royal entourage while the Argonauts and the crew got away with the Golden Fleece. In some versions of the legend, the murder of Medea's brother, Absyrtus, is incredibly violent. One account involves her cutting up the body and scattering it across her father's lands in the knowledge that he would spend time retrieving each and every piece in order to provide his son with a proper burial. Other versions suggest that Absyrtus was pursuing Jason and Medea before Jason himself committed the murder. In this version, one of Jason's crew named Atalanta was injured but was healed by Medea's magical abilities. Certain authors include the detail that the escaping crew stopped on the island owned by Circe, Medea's aunt, who cleansed them of their sins. There was a clear belief in the violent, negative capabilities of the witch Medea, who was willing to murder her brother to foster her escape. Throughout the rest of Jason's story, throughout his journey home and his celebration of the retrieval of the Golden Fleece, Medea was an ever-present. Her trickery and cunning helped the crew out of a number of scrapes, while her skill with healing potions helped to heal Jason's father.

Once the group arrived back at home, Golden Fleece in hand, the ruling king refused to give up the throne that rightfully belonged to Jason. Medea conspired to have the king, Pelias, moved aside to make way for the man she loved. Not only did she want to get him out of the way, but she also decided to use her magical abilities to have Pelias's own daughters kill him. To do this, she told the girls that she could transform an old ram into a much younger ram simply by cutting up the older animal and boiling it in a magical broth infused with herbs. As the girls watched, they saw a ram jumping around the pot. Caught up in the moment, they captured the ram and cut him up, putting him in the pot. But Medea has used her skills to disguise Pelias. The daughters, certain they were butchering a ram, instead dismembered their own father. Once it became clear what Medea had done, she and Jason ran away once again, this time fleeing to Corinth. They spent the next ten years together, bringing five sons into the world.

At this point, we have seen just how destructive and fearsome Medea's powers can be. The Ancient Greeks believed, clearly, that a witch's powers would have such a comprehensive influence over a person that they could encourage daughters to kill their own father. The combination of regicide and patricide incumbent in the story gives an immoral edge and seems to warn people of the corrupting influence of witches and magic in general. In addition to this, the manner in which Medea treated Jason's father's infirmity is something of a precursor to modern medicine. She used a blood transfusion to return life and vigor to the man thousands of years before doctors were able to carry out such a procedure. Even in the ancient times, the witch's healing abilities were well-known and misunderstood. But the story does not end with Medea and Jason settling down with their family. Instead, there is a darker end, one that Euripides seems to use as a cautionary tale against the powers held by witches.

In Corinth, after Jason and Medea had spent a decade together, things took a turn for the worst. Jason's attention was caught by the daughter of a local king. This girl, named Glauce, was younger and more beautiful than Medea and stole Jason away. Furious and desperate for revenge, Medea devised a plan. She sent Glauce a set of gifts, a dress and a coronet made of gold. But rather than simple presents, both were coated in poison. The trap was enough to not only kill Glauce, but also her father – the king – as well. Medea enlisted the help of two of her sons in carrying out the act, a pair who were caught by the locals and put to death. But the killing of Glauce and her father was not enough. Driven into a rage, Medea killed two more of her children, leaving only one son left alive. This son, Thessalus, was the sole surviving product of the bond between Jason and Medea. For some writers, the killing of Medea's children at her own hand was an accident, while others have told the story as though the children died as a result of her vengeful actions. It is Euripides and later writers who attribute the murder directly to Medea the witch.

When Jason discovered the death of his new love and his children, he is enraged. Medea, knowing this would occur, had already fled the country. She tried to hide in Thebes, before being driven out by the locals. Moving then to Athens, she met a man named Aegeus and, together, they had a son. When Aegeus's long-lost son – Theseus, himself a well-known figure – returned home, Medea was the only one to recognize his true identity and felt that her own son's position was threatened. She convinced her new husband that he must kill Theseus and even devised a plan to use poison to accomplish her goal. Aegeus, just before murdering Theseus, realized his real identity and threw the cup of poison to the floor. Medea's plot was foiled, and once again, she had to flee the city. Accounts differ in what happens next, but it seems as though Medea tried to return home, became embroiled in familial politics, and then fell into obscurity.

Even if her story might not have had the concise ending afforded to many of the heroes of Greek legend, the story of Medea tell us a lot about ancient views of witches. Her character is distinctive, forming our template for the image of witches throughout the ages. She is shown to have a mastery of potions and spells, to be able to hold her own against some of the greatest heroes of the age, and to be an empathetic character capable of real love, both for her children and for Jason. But she is also violent and vindictive. She murders and deceives, using her powers to encourage people to carry out deeds they might never normally consider. She wields magic for her own purpose, rather than to fulfil some ideological cause. Capable of cunning, powerful spells, the idea of Medea, a lone female witch, is one that sets the foundation for much of the witches in the western world over the coming centuries. In this respect, it is very important to think about Medea when we encounter the other witches in this book. As we will find out, many of the misunderstandings and mistruths relating to witches seemingly can be traced back to age-old falsities that have been passed down throughout the ages. Even if Medea is nothing but a legend, the existence of her story tells us a huge amount about witches anyway.

Medea's spell

While we might not have any spells that have directly been attributed to Medea, we do have some archaeological evidence of the kinds of magic that were being used in Greco-Roman society. One of the most common was the use of curses. The idea of a curse – or of a cursed object – is one that we come across again and again. Sometimes, they were used as a means of protection on valuable objects. If these items were stolen or broken, then the offending person would be struck with a curse. The results of this curse could be numerous. They included illness, pestilence, poor luck, and even death. Sometimes, these curses were placed on books, guarding the knowledge they contained from prying eyes.

But curses were not exclusively dark. There could be light curses, as well. We know this thanks to the objects known as Cursing Tablets that have been recovered from dig sites. It seems as though the witches and other magical users of the age would attempt to trap and harness malevolent spirits inside these tablets. Using thin lead shapes, the witches would use their skills to trap the evil curses (or righteous blessing) inside the metal. This thin piece of lead would then be rolled up and sealed with nails driven through the middle. Once sealed shut, with the magical power trapped inside, these tablets were then thrown down wells, nailed to the walls of certain temples, or placed into the graves alongside the recently deceased.

We have since recovered some of these tablets, and it seems as though the curses have long since worn off.

Unfurling the lead, we can read their appeals to the gods, their detailed histories of the victims, or simply a name that the magical practitioner wished to curse. One of these, found in the Roman ruins in London, tells of how a person named Tretia Maria was cursed, how her life, memory, mind, liver, and lungs were to disappear, and how her thoughts, words, and memories were to be confused to the point where she could no longer hide secrets. While we might not see many cursing tablets in common use today, the idea has remained in use in many witchcraft circles.

In this instance, we will focus on benevolent use. To accomplish this simple, ancient spell, all you will need is a pencil, a piece of paper, and a pin. First, you will need to center yourself. Wait until midnight and sit quietly on your floor in a cross-legged position. Keep the person who you hope to bless in your mind and allow your thoughts to focus on them. Picture good things happening to them, all of the positive energy flowing into their life. When the picture in your mind's eye is clearest, write their name in the center of the piece of paper using the pencil. Roll it up tight and use the pin to seal it shut. Once it is sealed, you should hide the rolled-up paper away from sight. It is important that no one else sees it. After some time, the positive energy you sealed in the scroll should flood outwards into the wider world and begin to affect your desired target. Once you feel the spell is complete, take the paper, remove the pin, and burn the paper. This should only be done once or twice a year, lest it lose its effectiveness.

Agnes Sampson

The fear of witches has long been indicative of how they are viewed by the world. Throughout this text, we will see again and again how the fear of witchcraft and dark magic in general has colored the perception of those who (rightly or wrongly) have been accused of witchcraft. Just as Medea's story forms the backbone of our modern cultural perception of what witches can accomplish, the persecution of witches that we have seen across the centuries can be traced back to legends such as those Greek stories. In the case of Agnes Sampson, we will encounter one of the first examples of the notorious witch trials, set in the strange and twisted world of Scotland in the 1500s.

At the time, Scotland was a strikingly different place from today. As can be expected from European countries at the time, religion was a large part of day-to-day life, with the Catholic and Protestant schism continuing to assert itself on a regular basis. The ruling king, James VI, was a Protestant, but in the early stages of his life, his Christian leanings seemed not to prevent him from taking a more unconcerned approach to the toleration of witchcraft and the rumors of magic being practiced in his kingdom. This would not last, however, and the key change came when James was adventuring abroad, taking a ship to visit Copenhagen. During the voyage, the boat was beset by strong and worrying storms. Forced to take shelter along the Danish coast, James used the time in Denmark to kindle an interest in witchcraft. Denmark, unlike Scotland, was a country familiar with the concept of witch trials and a country that was in the thrall of such investigations. These matters piqued the interest of the Scottish king, who began to learn more and more from his hosts.

When quizzing his Danish hosts about the storms that continued to besiege his vessel whenever he tried to sail anywhere, James was told that the inclement weather was the result of the work of witches. Whereas James had previously considered witches to be a harmless oddity associated with the country and ancient pagan practices, his view began to change. As he spent more time in Denmark and was increasingly told about the power witches possessed, his opinions on magical practitioners were shaped by the Danes. By the time he returned to his home country, James was resolute in his decision to combat witchcraft at every opportunity. For any witches practicing in Scotland in the 1500s, their lives would be forever altered by James's fateful voyage. When he returned to Scotland, James attended the North Berwick witch trails. Though common in other countries throughout Europe, this was the first large-scale, organized prosecution of witches to take place in Scotland. Thanks to a law that had passed nearly a century earlier – the Witchcraft Act of 1563 – the courts held the power to question, prosecute, and eventually punish those it found guilty of witchcraft. The subject matter had been something of an obsession for the king, who would even write Daemonologie in 1597, an exploration of his views and comprehensions of the magical arts. While the laws had been left largely ignored during James's reign, his newfound vigor for the uncovering of magical practitioners changed the landscape of Scotland. The first investigations were held to look into those who had supposedly turned the weather against the king's ship. Many women were rounded up and questioned, among them one woman known as Agnes Simpson.

Agnes was a girl from a small town in Scotland. She was from a part of the country known as East Lothian on the northern shore, not quite the wilderness and stormy weather one might find up in the Highlands. Growing up in the area all of her life, she gradually began to develop a reputation as something of a healer. Like many of the women accused of witchcraft at the time, she was the town's recognized midwife, helping women with their pregnancies and assisting with the birth of most everyone in the town. Her knowledge about such matters might not have been magical in itself, but it was beyond the realm of understanding for the majority of people in the 15th and 16th centuries. As a midwife, she was thought to have seemingly strange and magical powers, including the ability to heal women in some of the most delicate positions. She fulfilled an important role in her local society and was relied upon by many. But this position of trust was not to last.

Following King James's fateful voyage to Denmark, he bought back with him both a new wife – Anne – and the Danish court's obsession with tracking down and punishing witches. Agnes was not the first to fall victim to the Witchcraft Act. In 1590, a young girl named Gilly Duncan was working as a servant in the town of Tranent, near Edinburgh. She was arrested under the suspicion of being a witch, being accused of handing out cures to heal people. These cures had been the subject of many rumors and had been labelled miraculous by some, with others taking this information and deducing that the girl must be a witch. Despite Gilly's protestations to the contrary and an outright refusal to admit that she had been in any way involved in a pact with the devil, Gilly was tortured and questioned. When being examined by the prosecutors, she was found to bear a "devil's mark," an area of supposedly tainted or discolored skin on her neck that marked out her agreement with Satan. After the intense pressure from the authorities, she finally relented and admitted to her involvement with the dark powers. According to her confession, Gilly admitted to being a witch and to selling her soul to the devil. This was the pact that provided her with such wonderful cures. Subjected to even more torture, she was asked to name names. Among the people she named were a local male schoolteacher thought to be a wizard, the widow of an archbishop, the 1st Earl of Bothwell, the daughter of a lord, and Agnes Sampson, the local midwife. After her confession was finally deemed suitable, Gilly was burned alive at the stake.

Following Gilly's confessions and execution, close to seventy people were rounded up under the suspicion of being involved in witchcraft in some way. Of these, many were executed, though we don't have any means of checking exact numbers. Before they were executed, many of these people were given the same treatment as Gilly and faced torture. There were allegations that a group of witches (a coven) had been meeting in the churchyard in North Berwick during certain nights and had therein dedicated themselves to the evil arts. Of the various plots that had been put forward at the churchyard, it was said that the group had plotted to poison the king and various members of his household, as well as casting the spell that had sent the bad weather after the king's ship. One of the most notorious confessions extracted by the torturers related to an event on Halloween in 1590, when the group of witches were said to have acted upon the devil's instruction and dug up recently buried bodies, removed a number of organs and limbs from each, and then attached them to a dead cat. This chimera was then thrown into the sea, the very spell that was thought to have caused the storms plaguing James's journey. A frequent claim during the torture sessions was that the devil was obsessed with King James, whom he (the devil) considered his greatest enemy. Such a claim flattered the king and condemned the accused.

But it is the case of Agnes Sampson that lingers longest in the memory. By the time the widespread witch trials lurched into motion, the entire country seemed to be beset by a fever. Led by the king himself and his new Danish wife, there was a compulsion to track down and burn witches wherever they could be found. The way the accusations had been interpreted, it seemed as though the authorities believed Agnes to be among the highest ranking and most powerful of the suspected witches in Scotland. As such, she was personally brought before the king so that he might be able to examine her himself. Faced by the woman who had supposedly cursed the weather during his voyage, James took a special interest in the trial of Agnes. Despite the best efforts of the king and his court in examining the midwife, no one could force her to confess to the crimes she was said to have committed. At every turn, Agnes denied being involved. So she was taken away to the dungeons, and like many of the other accused witches, was subjected to a regime of brutal torture.

The method of discovering which of the accused were truly in league with the devil often came down, as in the case of Gilly, to those who bore the "devil's mark." This was said to be the place where Satan himself had licked the witch and brought her into his power. Just as with Gilly, such a mark was found on the tortured body of Agnes and was taken to be proof enough of the accused having been in collusion with the dark arts. Agnes's mark was only found when her jailors shaved away all of her hair and examined her bald body. At this point, James was still unsure as the potential guilt of Agnes. Having examined her himself and after hearing tales of the torture chamber, he wondered how anyone could withhold the truth. One of the torture items used on Agnes was known as the witch's bridle. It was an iron tool fixed with four sharp spikes. Placed around the head, the spikes forced themselves into the subject's mouth. Two were pressed directly on to the tongue, while the remaining two jutted sharply into the victim's cheeks. This was how the subject was left, prevented from moving too much less they be cut by the bridle, unable to sleep. It was only after being in the bridle for so long, with a rope around her neck, and in conjunction with the search for the devil's mark, that Agnes finally broke down and confessed to her sins.

Agnes Sampson eventually confessed to 563 counts of witchcraft. She was taken directly from the dungeons of the castle, strangled with a rope, and then burned at the stake. The date at the time of her death was the 16th of January, 1591, with the execution notice even going so far as to note the cost of the entire enterprise. To kill Agnes Sampson as a witch, to force her confession, had taken weeks of torture and the cost of £6, 8s, and 10d. To this day, it is said that the ghost of the dead witch haunts the corridors of Holyrood Palace, where she had met with King James. The ghost, naked and bald, howls in the face of those she encounters, furious about the fate that befell her.

The story of Agnes Sampson is very typical of many case of witches or women falsely accused of witchcraft. The skills she provided, whether magical or simply a result of a deep connection with nature and a fine knowledge of the local plants and ancient cures, were strange enough to those around her that she was deemed to be magical. Unfortunately for Agnes, these skills that had helped so many people in her town would eventually become her undoing. Regardless of whether she was a witch or not, the execution of Agnes Sampson teaches us just how society often reacts to the possibility of magic in a community.

Agnes' spell

Agnes did not leave behind any of her spells (or indeed, any indication that the accusations were true), but we do have a number of healing spells from the days when she was practicing. We know that she was primarily a healer and that her ability to help people in this respect was prodigious enough to at least be accused of magical knowledge. One of the best spells that we have from that time is known simply as The Witch's Ladder. It is a simple spell, but an ancient and powerful one when conducted correctly. In order to try it for yourself, you will need three types of rope. These can be anything: rope, string, yarn, wool. It has even been said that using the hair of an intended target can make the spell even more powerful. For now, it might be worth first trying it out with whatever you have lying around the home.

The first step is to ensure you have the right tools. Once you have gathered them together and have found a set of three individual (but different) pieces that work for you, then you can reuse them again and again. You can even carry them around with you. The process of casting this spell is relatively simple and often crops up in other, more complicated incantations. The witch's ladders have been compared to rosary beads in the past in their cathartic properties and the comfort many people derive from having them close.

As mentioned before, the process is very simple. Take all three lengths of cord/rope/string/whatever you have and hold them firmly at either end. Give them a little twist so that there's a spiral effect and then release one hand. Now, begin to tie knots in the string. As you tie knots all along the length of the ropes, you should begin to say an incantation out loud. The words are the following:

> The knot of one, the spell begun
> The knot of two, that it comes true
> The knot of three, so that it may be
> The knot of four, more powerful than before
> The knot of five, to keep magic alive
> The knot of six, with the power to fix
> The knot of seven, calls on heaven
> The knot of eight, a challenge to fate
> The knot of nine, at last it's mine.

Say the words as you reach each knot. Ideally, you would place nine knots into the ladder, saying the relevant part of the incantation as you do so. As you say the words, however, it is important to keep in mind your overall goal. As we are casting a healing spell, then you should be focused on the potential to heal. Imagine the beneficiary (whether that is you or another person) becoming healed and well. By the time the knots are in place and the spell is cast, then the powers will be secured inside the ladder, bound in place by the knots. From here, it is possible to do whatever you want with the ladder. Some keep it in a bag, some keep it beside their bed. Others have been known to transform their ladder into a necklace, while others have given it as a gift.

The final part of the spell is important. Once the ladder has been tied, you must begin to untie the knots one day at a time. On the first day, for example, untie the first knot. Do so once a day, for nine days, until you have released all of the energy from the ladder. Once this is done, then the spell has been cast. Typically, it is best to only cast the spell once a month, less you drain the power from yourself.

Alice Kyteler

Despite how the case of Agnes Sampson might appear, not every accusation of witchcraft was levelled at a nice old woman who just happened to possess untold knowledge. In the case of Alice Kyteler, we will be travelling back a little further in time and examining what might be one of the first trials of witchcraft in Europe. Taking place in Ireland during the fourteenth century, the trial of Alice Kyteler was a landmark case in the treatment of witches in recorded history. It is also an example of a woman who certainly sailed close to the negative side of the moral spectrum. Many took the accusations levelled against Alice, certainly far from an angel, as being true simply because of her dubious past.

Born as early as 1280, Alice Kyteler was not poor. Instead, she was born in her family's household in Kilkenny, an established Anglo-Saxon family who lived in the area. By the time she grew up, she was known as

Dame Alice Kyteler, assuming her position as a powerful woman with considerable wealth. As the only child in her family, she was the chief benefactor of the inheritance that passed down to her. The money, the lands, and the title were far and away more than was available to the majority of people in medieval Ireland. Despite this, it did not protect her from the suspicions of the townsfolk.

Perhaps one of the most suspicious elements of Alice's past – and one that is often used as evidence in her dubious moral past – is her history as a married woman. In all, she was married four times to four different men, all of whom died in fairly strange circumstances. We should start at the beginning, with a man named William Outlaw. William was a merchant and one of the most important money lenders in Kilkenny. The pair were married for a number of years, during which time they had a son together, also named William. They might have also had a daughter, though this has never been confirmed. However, the marriage did not last. William died suddenly, and it was not long before Alice was married again, this time to Adam Blund, another money lender, who hailed from Callan. In 1302, Adam and Alice faced accusations from people who believed that they had worked together to kill William. She was already not a popular figure because of the fortunes she had inherited and her heavy involvement in the world of extortionate money lending, and many were quick to believe the rumors.

Despite the fact that Alice and Adam survived these damaging rumors, Adam did not last long. He, too, met his end in a strange fashion. Again, it was not long before Alice found herself a new partner. This time she got engaged to Richard Valle. A landholder from a neighboring county, he was not averse to marrying a widow, especially seeing as the rumors about her previous husbands had not made their way to County Tipperary. Nevertheless, Alice, as a widow, was required to pay her own dowry. She did this as she was still a wealthy woman, and – perhaps – she knew that the death of Richard Valle was not too far away. Eventually, Richard met the same fate and was added to the list of former husbands of Alice Kyteler.

Alice's final husband was a man named John le Poer. John was more informed than the previous husbands as to his new wife's past, and when he began to fall ill, he was the one who led the accusations against Alice and accused her of poisoning him and hoping him dead. In his opinion, Alice was a murderer. She used poison, and most worryingly of all, sorcery and magic in order to kill her string of husbands. Now, she was attempting to do the same to him. The one man who she had not tried to kill was her first son, William, whom John accused her of favoring at all times. John died, but not before his accusations had been heard by his children, who in turn passed on the information to the family members of the previous husbands with whom Alice had been involved. Together, they gathered and formulated their theories. Aside from the murderous charges they levelled against her, Alice was also accused of repeatedly rejecting the church and Christ Himself, of killing and dismembering animals to use in sacrifices to demons she met at crossroads, of holding meetings during the night in churches in which she performed dark magic, of using her powers and her potions to exert control over good Christian people, of possessing a "familiar" – a lesser demon – named Robin Artison as her companion, and of conspiring against the men she married.

Possibly because the rumors had circulated around Alice for so long, people were more than willing to believe that she might be involved in the practice of witchcraft. Alice was either incredibly unlucky in her choice of husbands, or she did indeed have a murderous streak in her character. But by this stage, the truth did not entirely matter. By the death of John le Poer and the meetings between her former families, the fame of Alice's case had spread. One of the people who heard the story was Richard de Ledrede, who was the Bishop of Ossory. He was known as a man obsessed with morality and imposing the laws of the church onto others.

It was 1324 when the Bishop first got of the case. It was perfect for him; the chance to flex his clerical muscles and at the same time condemn the practice of witchcraft, which had begun to worry him with increasing regularity. Alice herself seemed unperturbed by the accusations, hoping to dust them off and ignore any truth that might lie behind the words of her enemies. She resisted when the Bishop of Ossory began to make moves to have her arrested, and used her powerful and wealthy position to drive him away. She called in favors from friends and ensured that she remained untouchable by the church.

Rather than Alice Kyteler being arrested, it was the Bishop who was thrown in jail. De Ledrede was imprisoned and faced questioning by the ruler of Kilkenny, who wondered why he had the audacity to attack and accuse a powerful noble woman. Dame Alice Kyteler, it seemed, knew the right people and knew who would best be able to assist her. But there was little that could be done to hold the Bishop of Ossory in jail. He was eventually released, and having had his fascination piqued by the case, continued to campaign for the arrest of the multiple widow. Gearing up to make the case even more famous, the bishop's vigor is demonstrative of the changing wave of public perception towards witches that would soon spread across the continent.

One of the most important actions carried out by the bishop was the decision to write to Roger Utlagh, who was the Chancellor of Ireland and the country's ruling authority. The letter he sent demanded that Alice be arrested for her actions and put forward the case for the suspected witchcraft that had taken place. A key argument by the bishop was that Alice's actions were a threat to the faith. A law passed in Ireland, named *Ut inquisitions,* was passed in 1298 and called upon the secular authorities to cave to the whims of the church. This would be one of the key interpretations of the law during Alice's trial. Without much in the way of legal precedent when it came to trying witches, laws such as these were repurposed to achieve the goals of the clergy.

But the case was not entirely clear cut. Alice, a noble woman, was actually related to the Chancellor of Ireland through the family tree of one of her dead husbands. The Chancellor, not wishing to bring any scurrilous rumors to light pertaining to his family, asked the Bishop of Ossory to drop the case as a personal favor. While he failed to get the bishop to drop the case, he did manage to delay the trial. This allowed Alice to make an escape, and before the bishop could get to her, she ran to the home of Roger Ultagh. On learning what had happened, the bishop accused the Chancellor of protecting the heretical woman and allowing witchcraft to flourish in Ireland.

The two competing authorities found themselves in a position of stalemate. The Chancellor was unwilling to allow his family member to be prosecuted as a witch (regardless of her actual crimes), while the bishop was fervent in his desire to see Alice tried. And so the bishop took an alternative tack. He instead arrested a member of Alice's household, taking into his control a female servant named Petronella de Meath. This girl was tortured by the cleric, and a confession was extracted from her, Petronella eventually admitting to practicing witchcraft and doing so with Alice Kyteler. This was the confession the bishop needed, but he wanted more. He continued to go after the members of Alice's household, capturing more and more of them and eliciting confessions of witchcraft from each. Petronella did not escape further punishment. She was publically whipped, attached to a stake, and then burned alive in November of 1324. Alice was worried, and along with Petronella's daughter, fled again. In her place, the authorities turned to her first son, William, against whom they levied similar accusations, including heresy, adultery, perjury, and even killing a priest. William renounced these sins and was not put to death. Not necessarily accused of witchcraft, he got away with simply having to attend mass three times a day and spend long time assisting the local poor.

The attempted prosecution of Alice Kyteler is not necessarily important because she was such a powerful witch. Rather, it shows a very early example of the willingness of people (and in particular, the clergy) to mix the strange and possibly immoral actions of one woman with the idea that she might be a witch. Over the coming centuries, more and more women would face accusations of being witches when in fact they were simply not trusted, were suspected, or were otherwise not liked. It's important to be able to notice the difference between women in this text who are persecuted for their magical activities and those who are persecuted for other actions. In the end, Alice managed to escape, but not everyone had her money or influence. Indeed, her servant suffered a hideous fate and it could be argued that she took the blame for the possible murders committed by her employer. While it is unlikely that Alice Kyteler was a witch in the sense that we might like to think of witches, she was nevertheless part of the propaganda campaign to liken any kind of suspicious female activity with the dark arts. As we will see later in this book, this often meant the death of women who were not witches and the escape of actual magic users who managed to escape the attention of the authorities for whatever reason.

Alice's spell

Had it been proven that Alice Kyteler was actually a witch who was using her powers to kill a succession of husbands, it would be unbecoming to share the exact spell with the readers of this book. Instead, we will take a similar kind of magic to what she might have been using and work on an ancient concoction that is designed to heal, rather than harm.

The healing power of green tea has been long documented and is seen in a number of different cultures, from Europe to Asia. In this spell, we will discover how teas such as this one can be used to cast a spell designed to increase financial wellbeing and to heal any kind of money hemorrhaging that might be occurring in your life.

The first step, as might be obvious, is to make a pot of green tea. It is better to use the freshest ingredient as possible. Any amount of tea will suffice in some capacity. The trick is to use a teapot, rather than just a single cup. Once the water is boiled, begin to steep the tea and allow it to brew. You will also need two green candles and a part of the home where you can sit and be still for a while.

Once the tea is steeping, take the pot and place it before the space where you will be sitting. Set up the two candles on either side of the pot and sit in front of them. Before you light anything, kneel forward and hold your hands over the steaming pot of tea. Allow the steam to rise up between your fingers and notice how the escaping vapors intermingle with your fingers. Focus your energies through the fingers and begin to chant the following to yourself:

Oh, gods of far and gods of near,
Enter into the space I hold dear.
Remove any shades and slights against myself,
Allow me to enjoy the coming of wealth.

The spell should serve to concentrate the energies that you feel and wish to impart to the tea. Once you are finished, light the candles (left, then right) and then sit back before the tea. Give yourself a few minutes to dwell upon the idea of wealth entering into your life and then when it is cool enough, pour yourself a cup of the green tea and drink it. You should be able to feel the warmth radiating through your body as you do so. Once the cup is finished, put out both of the candles (left, then right) and then clear away everything. Over the coming weeks, you should begin to notice more and more opportunities in your life in which you might be able to capitalize and attract wealth towards yourself. Just as Alice was protected by her wealth, you might find that this kind of spell becomes very useful for you.

Marie Laveau

We have looked at cases from hundreds of years ago thus far. But there is always an interest in the strange and the magical. During this next chapter, we will look into the life of a woman whose existence was closer to modern times and whose magic was further from what we think we might know. The name "witch" has been applied to many people, but few of them are exactly alike. While it might bring to mind the idea of a Halloween-decoration-style old woman with a hooked nose and a wide-brimmed hat, there are many other types of magical practitioner. Marie Laveau, our next subject, is commonly held to be the Queen of Voodoo. For this entry, we will travel to the New World, specifically New Orleans in the early 19th Century.

The French Quarter of New Orleans is still one of the strangest places in America. Though it is much more of a tourist destination these days, it has long held a reputation as being somewhere mysterious. Perhaps this is due to the history of the city and its combination of cultures that have met on that exact spot. Not only are the French and American influences well represented and obvious, but also the history of the Haitians and other former slaves in the city add up to a truly unique local culture. This was the case in the late 1700s as much as it is today.

We have very little information about the early life of Marie Laveau. We know that she was born as a free woman during the latter stages of the 18th Century in the French Quarter of the city of New Orleans. Her mother was a Creole, who themselves were a blend of the Spanish and French inhabitants of the Louisiana colony. Her father, Charles Laveau, was a powerful man in the city and was the fifth person to be elected mayor. Of Marie's early life, there is not much in the way of information. It seems apparent that she would not have wanted for much, and that she was born into a very strange time for the city. Increasingly, the original cultural make-up of New Orleans was changing. As well as the new-founded American spirit, there were elements of British culture married to the Spanish and French, as well as the importation of Caribbean and African cultures in the form of the slave trade that was established and thriving in the city.

Marie grew up leaving little impact on the city records and seemingly doing little of note during this time. As might be expected for a young woman, she got married. Meeting a man named Jacques Paris, she married in 1819. Jacques had been born in Haiti, and unlike the majority of the high society in New Orleans, was not white. Their marriage is one of the first credible facts we have about Marie, with the marriage certificate still in the records of the St Louis Cathedral, still present in the city. Thanks to this document, we know that the ceremony at the wedding was conducted by Father Antonio de Sedella, with the help of a priest named Pere Antoine.

But the marriage did not last long. Just a year later, Marie lost her Haitian husband. The records of the death of Jacques Paris indicate that he passed away in 1820. Jacques was part of a wider movement of Haitian emigration, a movement that brought hundreds of his fellow countrymen to the city in 1809, following the Haitian Revolution. This movement brought both the white slave owners, the black slaves, and the free people of color who were living on the island. They brought with them the Haitian culture, a mishmash of imported African slaves, local Haitans, and French owners. Hidden away in many other aspects of their culture was the magical practice of Voodoo. This would be one of the key elements that the Haitian emigration would bring to New Orleans. Having spent a year with her Haitian husband, Marie Laveau was exposed to not only the various elements of Jacques's culture, but also the concepts of Voodoo. Once in New Orleans, many of the Haitians began to practice the art, and Marie found herself suddenly thrust into a strange new world.

What we do know about Marie's life as a widow is that she was not alone. In the short time that she had spent with Jacques, the pair had conceived a child (named after Marie). Together, the pair sank deeper and deeper into the New Orleans underground, moving away from the seemingly high society position Marie had held at birth as the daughter of a mayor and vanishing into the Haitian culture of Marie's late husband. During this time, it was thought that Marie grew more and more familiar with the practice of Voodoo. It's long been told that one of the key tenets of this strange, magical art is the ability to bring people back from the dead, information that some people have thought meant that Marie was searching for a way to revive her husband.

Despite vanishing from the public eye, Marie and her daughter still needed money. It was decided that Marie would use her newfound skills in an attempt to raise some cash for the small family. The child Marie was trusted with the responsibility off hosting these events. Still a growing girl, she would show off the skills that her dedicated, magical mother was beginning to pass down. Through these performances on the street and at parties and carnivals, the pair were able to receive some measure of financial support. More importantly, it helped to cement Marie's reputation as the Voodoo Queen in New Orleans. By blending together the Roman Catholicism of her youth with the Haitian Voodoo of her late husband, she established a reputation and a practice as one of the most powerful witches in North America. A far cry from the classic idea of witches riding broomsticks and dressed all in black, Marie's own magic was a particularly localized version of the magical arts.

As such, Marie's work in New Orleans composed a great deal of what we know about Voodoo today. Her approach was important, being as she was the self-stylized Voodoo Queen in a city with perhaps the biggest magical influence in the United States. That's not to say that everyone was a fan of the arts she was practicing. Years later, when her daughter followed in her footsteps, she was forced to send her children abroad. All three were sent to the Dominican Republic to prevent people from acting out on their threats to burn the children alive. Instead, all three travelled to the Dominican Republic and were raised in the Voodoo tradition.

But for Marie Laveau, life was a tricky affair. She needed to walk the line between a legitimate method of making money and still practicing Voodoo as she pleased. This is perhaps why we have records of her as a liquor importer in New Orleans, as well as legends that say she was a hairdresser working for clients of a high social standing. Both careers would potentially give her an excellent cover story for her magic, particularly the latter. Very few people would question the idea of a high-priced hairdresser visiting the homes of her well-known clients in order to provide the very best services around. Rather, if Marie was using the opportunity to carry out Voodoo rituals, then few people would have suspected. Likewise, a position as a hairdresser might have provided Marie with an excellent opportunity to find out private information about members of the New Orleans high society, thus protecting herself even more if the authorities should come knocking on her door.

In New Orleans, a well-known legend about Marie is her snake. A central part of Voodoo folklore, the snake appears in both stories and spells for a number of reasons. Marie kept the animal as a "familiar," a trusted servant who was never seen far from its master. She named it Zombi, the name given to a traditional African god and one of the most notorious legends in Voodoo culture. To many, a zombie is the reanimated corpse of a deceased person, imbued with life thanks to the power of the Voodoo magic. To some, this was an indication that Marie had somehow managed to revive the spirit of her dead husband and place it inside her familiar. But she never talked about the practicalities of the animal, and like much of Marie's life, the creature is shrouded in mystery.

One of the most defining aspects of Marie's particular brand of magic was the unique cross section between two major cultures. Marie, raised a Roman Catholic, was exposed to the Haitian and African practices of Voodoo by her late husband. In combining both of these religions, she seemed to draw on power from both. Her interpretation of traditional Voodoo involves invoking the power of the Catholic saints in order to achieve a greater level of power. Though this is now a regular feature for many common practitioners, it is thought that Marie was the key figure in cultivating a modern, blended version of ancient Voodoo rituals.

For Marie, however, one of the major sources of her power was not in magic, but rather in information. As we have mentioned already, she used positions such as a possible career as a hairdresser in order to draw out information about the high ranking members of the city's society. As a member of the upper classes herself, she knew how to move among these circles and how each group overlapped with one another. She knew the major players, which people could be best pressed for information, and where she might best send any knowledge she knew. As an information broker, she was easily one of the most powerful women in New Orleans at the time. But her magical arts gave her another life. Thanks to her skills with Voodoo, she was able to move in all kinds of social circles. She was well known and loved among the Haitian communities and could move through the New Orleans underworld without anyone raising an eyebrow. Her reputation as the Queen of Voodoo gave her protection and meant that few people would ever consider betraying her. Mastering both the high and low strata of society in New Orleans, she could use the information she possessed as a currency. It would be possible to exchange knowledge for influence and favors, while relying on her magical skills as a form of back-up. She could use Voodoo to intimidate the servants of a household or to pressure the home owners with her knowledge of their most private affairs. With so much power, it is no wonder that she was so feared and so respected at the same time.

Despite her reputation, there was nothing that Marie could do to avoid her own death. Most of the information we have about her demise is gathered from her obituary, printed in the Daily Picayune, a New Orleans newspaper. The short piece announces that she died a peaceful death at her home. Typically, this is where the story would end, but there are two things worth noting. The first is that Marie was one of the few witches in this book who was permitted a peaceful death on her own terms. This is perhaps an indicator of the amount of true power that she held, that the authorities were afraid to challenge her. Secondly, a number of reports from around the city mentioned seeing Marie in the weeks following her death on the 17th of June, 1881. Difficult to confirm, these independent reports together add one final element of mystery to the story. Voodoo did not perish in the Laveau family upon Marie's death. Instead, it was carried on through her descendants. Along with many other pupils and students she taught, the influence of Marie Laveau ensured that New Orleans would forever be associated with its own particular brand of Voodoo and home to a very particular type of witch.

Marie's spell

As Marie was so heavily involved in the world of Voodoo, it is only right that we should spend some time learning some of the skills that made her such a powerful figure. While it would be impossible to replicate the breadth of information that she wielded in local society, we can at least attempt a Voodoo spell. For any burgeoning magic user, learning about the full range of abilities in the world of magic is essential. With that in mind, this spell – particular to New Orleans – should help you to banish any magical, negative barriers that you feel in your life.

Ask anyone about Voodoo, and one of the most commons replies will concern the small dolls that have been so heavily linked to the art. These dolls, however, and their ability to influence and affect real people, take a great deal of skill and involve many questions concerning the morality of magic. Instead, we will focus on the ability to tear down those energy-based barriers that can so often appear in our lives and prevent us from achieving our goals. For this spell, we will need some dark rum, a shard of broken glass, a ceramic bowl, and four (very hot) chilies.

First, turn off all the lights in a room. Wait until midnight, when the moon is full and the clouds are absent. Ensure that enough of the moonlight is pouring into the room so that you may see what you are doing. Place the tools in front of you. Next, announce your intentions to the room. Any spirits that are listening will hear you when you tell them about the barriers that you feel are present in your life. Explain how they are inhibiting you (whether this is in your love life, your career, or in any other aspect of your being). It is important to announce yourself confidently, so it can be worth rehearsing your words before you begin and having a very firm idea in your mind of exactly what barriers are causing you trouble.

Next, place the shard of glass into the bottom of the bowl. Place the four chilies on top (you may wish to wear gloves if they are particularly strong), and then dribble in the dark rum on top of both. Pour in enough to cover the chilies. Wave your right hand over the bowl, and then drink some of the rum for yourself. Once this is done, you must take the bowl outside and place it beneath a tree as an offering. The best results are gained with larger trees. Leave it there for the night. At dawn, return to the bowl, and empty out the contents at the foot of the tree so that it seeps into the earth. The spell is now complete, and you should find that the barriers in your life slowly begin to crumble. It has been noted that some people experience better results depending on the type of chilies they use and the strength and darkness of the rum. You may wish to experiment with a number of different types if you are not finding the right results.

Merga Bien

While Marie Laveau might have been able to turn her powers into something resembling real political influence, not every woman accused of witchcraft has been quite so lucky. As we have already seen in this book, some of the worst victims of the campaign against witches by those who have misunderstood the premise have been subjected to the phenomena known as the witch trials. Taking place across Europe, these fanatic events saw the execution of a huge number of women and men. While some might indeed have been attempting to practice magical arts, there is no doubt that the executions resulted in the death of many innocent victims. In certain cases, as in the death of Merga Bien, the innocent victim was her unborn child, condemned by the association with its mother. Merga was accused of having sex with the devil and was therefore dragged before the highest courts in the land while still pregnant and told to answer to claims of dark magic. As we will see, the result was part of a wider process of systematic executions taking place in Germany at the time.

We have already seen – in the case of James VI of Scotland – how the particular fascination of those in power with the mysterious arts of witchcraft can end up being damning for anyone who has ever shown even the slightest interest in the practice. In 17th Century Germany, in a town named Fulda, we can see how this kind of obsession among those in power took a very real toll on the local women. Fulda is not much of a town. It demanded little attention in the day and – even in modern times – still fails to attract much fame. A cursory search for the town on the internet will no doubt drag up the very case we will be examining in the next chapter, demonstrating how cataclysmic and singular the famous Fulda witch trials were to the local population. Before we begin to look at Merga Bien herself, time should be taken to look into the history of the man who led the charges against her, a local prince named Balthasar von Dembach.

The events of this chapter take place in the year 1603 and last close to three years. During this time, 205 people are thought to have died, thanks to the campaign led by Prince Balthasar von Dembach. A stringent Catholic and part of the movement that hoped to counter the rise in Protestantism that had gripped northern Europe in the preceding century, Von Dembach saw it as his duty to destroy any semblance of anti-Christian (and anti-Catholic) behavior in his province. Elected by a panel of local lords, he was not only the Prince of the area, but also the local bishop. This imbued him with both a political and a religious authority, a power that he used to combat any kind of liberalism and movement away from the traditional teachings of the Catholic Church. Described by some as a fanatic, his re-election in 1602 can be taken as the beginning of the end for many of the people in the area. After having been exiled by the local community for a number of years, he returned with a renewed vigor and a dedication that would leave many people damaged in his wake.

Backed up by such radical Catholic ideas, Von Dembach saw it as his duty to the state and to God to rid the immediate vicinity of any kind of behavior he saw as bad. He picked a somewhat easy target, launching an investigation into all sorts of magic witchcraft, and sorcery that might have taken place in Fulda. In doing so, he hoped to purge any kind of irreligiousity from the town and demonstrate his faith to his electorate and his deity. After investigations were launched by the Prince-Bishop in March of 1603, arrests were made shortly thereafter. Among those arrested was a woman named Merga Bien.

Merga was, in many ways, a typical German woman of the day. Though her early life was not particularly of note – she certainly wasn't born into the moneyed backgrounds of other women like Alice Kyteler or Marie Laveau – she was nevertheless an interesting figure. One of the major pieces of information we have about her life before the witch trials is the fact that she had been married twice before 1588. Her first two husbands had died young and left the majority of their possessions to the widow. While one early death might seem normal in an age when medicine and antibiotics were not advanced, the death of the second husband began to turn heads. When she married a third man, Blasius Bien, in 1588, an increasing number of rumors began to travel across Fulda. There were suggestions that Merga was not quite the normal woman she appeared to be, that there might be something dark lurking beneath the surface. This was not a problem, however, as shortly after the marriage, Merga and Blasius moved to a new town in order to seek employment.

But the new job did not last long. Soon, after a falling out with Blasius's employer, Merga and her husband returned to Fulda. While she had been away, the rumors had only grown stronger, and the Prince Bishop Von Dernbach had been elected and launched his investigation. Unwittingly, Merga had thrown herself into a whirlwind of trouble. After the initial investigations were held in March, a wave of arrests followed. Merga herself was taken into custody on the 19th of June. This infuriated Blasius, who travelled to the nearby court in

Speyer to argue the case for his wife and to dissuade the authorities from believing that she might in any way be a witch.

A central part of Blasius's argument was that after being Merga's third husband for the last fourteen years, his wife was now finally pregnant. He thought that the courts might take mercy on a woman if they knew her to be with child, especially a conception that had taken the couple so long. What Blasius hadn't counted on was the extreme desire of the court to reach a conviction. Rather than seeing the new baby as a point in favor of allowing Merga to live, it was added to the accusations levied against her.

In all, Merga was accused of a number of magical conspiracies. To the court, working with the rumors that had been passed along from mouth to mouth, it seemed as though Merga had exercised her powers as a witch to kill both of her previous husbands. In doing so, she had been able to claim their inheritance for herself. After the claims were announced in the court, the Prince-Bishop's men took the accused and threw her into jail. Once imprisoned, Merga was subjected to the same treatment as many of the women in this book who were accused of witchcraft. She was brutally tortured, punished, and harmed until she finally relented and admitted to being involved in the dark magical arts.

This was exactly what the court had wanted to hear. The number of crimes Merga Bien was accused of was long. Not only had the court come across the rumors that she had murdered her second husband, but also that she might have killed children that sprang forth from her first marriages, and even potentially killed a man involved in Blasius's employment troubles. She had accomplished this, according to the courts, by conducting a black Sabbath. In league with the devil, she had summoned up the dark lord and pledged herself to do his bidding in return for great wealth and the power to kill.

Blasius was distraught. He found himself stuck arguing in front of the authorities, desperate to save his wife from execution. After fourteen years of marriage, the pair had finally managed to conceive a child. Typically, a pregnant woman might expect to have her execution commuted, at least until after the birth of the baby. But in this instance, the pregnancy was not Merga's saving grace, but rather the final nail in her coffin. After years of failing to conceive, the court argued that the newfound pregnancy was the result of even greater witchcraft. Rather than the child of Blasius, they were convinced that the child growing inside Merga was in fact the spawn of Satan himself. Rather than saving her life, the fact that she was pregnant after all these years was taken by the authorities as further proof that Merga must be a witch.

As a result, both Merga and her unborn child were sentenced to death. Whether Merga actually was involved in any form of witchcraft was never truly settled by the court. There have been suggestions that Merga turned to ancient knowledge in order to help her conceive. It might have been that old herbal remedies and actions for increasing one's fertility were used by the new wife, desperate to please her husband and finally settle down into married life after two early tragedies. These investigations into the ancient knowledge might have been all it took to interest the fanatical Prince-Bishop in her case and, combined with the rumors surrounding her first two marriages, led to the authorities to charge down her door. In the autumn of 1603, still pregnant, Merga Bien was put to death. Like so many other witches, she was burned at the stake. We may never know the extent of her true magical powers – whether her fertility spells actually worked – or indeed, whether she practiced witchcraft at all. She may even have killed her first two husbands. What we do know is that her execution took not only her life, but also the life inside her. To this day, Merga Bien's name is closely associated with some of the worst crimes committed during the hunt for witches during the 16th and 17th centuries.

Merga's spell

If we are to commemorate the memory of Merga Bien by learning one of her spells, then we should perhaps choose one that is most in line with what seems to have caused her ultimate demise. Fertility spells have long been a part of the canon of magic practiced by witches, and thankfully, it does not take a pact with Satan to encourage such an event. Instead, we can use knowledge and practices that have been passed down across the centuries in order to drum up a better chance of conceiving a child. While modern medicine should always be a first port of call when you are struggling to conceive, many of those who believe in the tenets of witchcraft believe that there is certainly some value in the elder knowledge and that it can be used to encourage the desired result.

In order to carry out this spell, you will need a number of household items. A traditional spell and one known to many older witches, it has for a long time been carried out not with specific magical items, but with the kind of objects we find surrounding ourselves in day-to-day life. These objects often have an inherent power that can be hard to match, especially if the household has been lived in for a long time. For a couple attempting to conceive, familiar objects are essential for the best fertility spells. We will require one hen's egg, a small pin, olive oil, a felt tip marker or paint brush, and a small straw basket. You will also need to find a body of moving water of any size.

Firstly, you should take the hen's egg and the pen or paint brush and begin to decorate the shell. You can draw any patterns you like, though it can help to look up your astrological sign and paint that. Some people choose to decorate the egg with images that mean something to them. Whatever you do, you will need to maintain the structural integrity of the egg. Don't break the shell. If you do, start again. Once you feel it is suitably decorated, then place the egg on a shelf in your bedroom and leave the ink to dry. It should remain in place for five days, ideally those in which the moon is approaching its fullest showing. When the five days are up and the moon is full, then you should wait until midnight of the fifth day. At that time, use the pin to puncture a small hole in the smaller tip of the egg. Place it upright (so that it does not leak), and then return it to the windowsill until morning.

The next day, take a few drops of your olive oil and dribble them over the opening in the egg. Once the oil has dried, take the egg and place it into the small straw basket. It should seem like something that is ready to float, a very light object. If you think it is too heavy, then you might need to rethink which basket you are using. The majority of small, straw baskets will indeed float. Next, take the egg and its basket to a body of moving water. Place the basket on the surface and watch as it floats away. Once it is out of sight, you should put it out of mind. In the coming days, you should continue to attempt to conceive. Ideally, the spell's energy will linger over your bedroom and will help with the process. As ever with medical matter, however, continued issues should always result in a visit to your doctor.

Agnes Waterhouse

The trial of Agnes Waterhouse is not only one of the most important in English history, but it also gives us a keen insight into the perception of the powers of witches in the 16th century. Thanks to the information that we still have from the trial, we can learn the details of the exact magic that the groups known as the Chelmsford witches were accused of carrying out as well as how they went about their arts. Though it differs widely from the magic that is often practiced in today's world, there are similarities and lessons to be learned from the entire trial. Agnes herself is typically given the top billing in the case, for it was she who became the first woman to be executed in England for the crime of witchcraft. However, the real story is far more complicated and involves other women who were attempting to practice magic.

Taking place in 1566, the court hearing was one of the first to have occurred in England following a change in the law with how witches were to be prosecuted. Queen Elizabeth I was sitting on the throne at the time, a woman whose father had caused major strife among the religious by turning the country away from Catholicism and toward the ideas borne out by the Reformation. Religious turmoil in the country was never far away, while stories about witches crept over the seas from Ireland and continental Europe. The Act of 1563 had recently been passed by parliament and was intended to tighten the penalties that were bestowed on those found guilty of practicing magic. Under the new legal framework, it was illegal to invoke any kind of evil spirit, whether harm resulted or not. A key element of the new rulings mentioned that the death penalty would not be invoked by the courts unless it could be proved that a human life had been removed due to the use of witchcraft. The trial of the Chelmsford witches would be the first to test these new laws.

Not only were the courts testing out new legalities, but those involved in the trial were famous in their own right. Taking place not far from the capital, the case was overseen by men such as John Southcote (a prestigious judge and member of the Royal Court), Reverend Thomas Cole, a local priest, Sir John Fortescue (who would go on to become Chancellor of the Exchequer), and Sir Gilbert Gerard (the Attorney General of England and a very famous man). Due to the involvement of these high ranking officials, and the fact that the trial was setting a legal precedent, the records were written up and distributed to courts around the country, offering advice on how they could prosecute similarly accused persons. As such, the majority of this chapter will take these records as source material.

In total, three women were pulled up before the court and had their crimes detailed for everyone to hear. They were Elizabeth Francis, Agnes Waterhouse, and Joan Waterhouse (Agnes's daughter). Together, they were all residents of a village named Hatfield Peverell and were only truly connected thanks to the existence of a large white cat that had been spotted with all three of them. According to other people in the village, the cat was a witch's familiar. Going by the name Satan (or Sathan), it was said to be able to talk. Of all the testimonies given in the court in Chelmsford, the most damning was that of a twelve-year-old girl, whose account delivered the final blow for Agnes.

But it was Elizabeth Francis who was first placed on trial. On the 26th of July, she appeared before the authorities accused of bewitching the baby of one of her neighbors. Belonging to a man named William Auger, the child is said to have become "decrepit" thanks to her magical influence. Elizabeth admitted to taking part in such an act, as well as accepting another string of accusations that went against her. Among the more nefarious of the crimes said to be carried out by the witch Elizabeth Francis were illegal abortions, murders, and adultery. She pled guilty to all.

Elizabeth said that she had received training in the art of witchcraft at a very young age. When she was twelve, her grandmother had begun to instruct her in the magical practices. Known as Mother Eve in the village, she had convinced Elizabeth to renounce the Christian God and enter into a pact with the devil. In order to do this, the young girl had to give blood to her new master. On receiving the offering, the devil came to the girl in the form of a large white cat. The animal demanded breakfast and milk and slept in the girl's kitchen for many years. It listened to Elizabeth's wishes (the first of which were apparently to have many possessions and riches) and promised to deliver. According to the records, the cat spoke with a strange and hollow voice. Acquiescing to the girl's first promise of receiving livestock, the cat delivered eighteen white-and-black sheep that appeared in the family's pasture one day.

Another demand of the familiar was that Elizabeth should have a husband; specifically, a man named Andrew Byles. A wealthy man about town, Elizabeth wanted him as her own. The cat promised to deliver, but only on the condition that the girl's new husband would be allowed to abuse his wife. She consented. Byles is known to have abused the girl, but then – according to the records – refused to marry Elizabeth. Furious, the girl went again to the cat and this time wished harm upon the man she had hoped to marry. She asked that the man's possessions be ruined and – when this came to pass – was not satisfied. Next, she asked that the devil might touch Byles and in doing so, kill him. This too came to pass. But carrying out such spells was not quite so simple. Every time Elizabeth placed a request to her familiar, she had to give something in return. To do this, she would prick her finger and mix drops of her blood in with the milk she fed to the cat. Eventually, red spots were seen across her body where she had repeatedly pricked herself.

After the death of Andrew Byles, Elizabeth believed herself to be pregnant. Not wishing to give birth to the man's son, she asked the cat to destroy the baby inside her. The cat responded with advice, telling her to seek out a certain herb that could be used to terminate the pregnancy (considered a crime in England at the time). Following this, the girl asked again for her husband. This time, the marriage went through, and though her new husband was not as wealthy as Andrew Byles, Elizabeth found herself content and pleased with herself. The couple soon had a child of their own, but before it was six months old, Elizabeth grew weary of its loud crying. She went again to her familiar and asked it to kill the child. The spell was carried out, the child died, but Elizabeth did not find the peace she desired. Lashing out at her husband, she tried to strike him lame. One day, when putting on his shoes, the man found a toad inside. Being told to kill the creature by his wife, he found himself struck by a lameness as soon as he touched the creature. This illness persisted for the rest of his days.

The large white cat was with Elizabeth for around fifteen years. During this time, she used its powers to carry out all manner of vicious and morally dubious spells. Each time, she pledged a little bit more of her blood to the creature. One day, the cat found itself with a new owner. Having been walking through the village, Elizabeth encountered Agnes Waterhouse. Knowing the old woman to be an excellent baker, Elizabeth asked her for a cake. In exchange, she promised to provide her with a magical item (though kept its real identity shrouded in mystery). Agnes saw this as a fair trade, agreeing to the deal. Once she received her cake, Elizabeth fetched Satan the white cat and passed her along to the old woman, teaching her exactly what she had learned from Mother Eve. The instructions she passed along included how to mix the blood with milk when casting a spell. For her crimes, the cat seemed to be forgiving towards Elizabeth Francis. She did not receive the death sentence despite the deaths she is thought to have caused, instead being imprisoned for a year.

Agnes Waterhouse, on trial the next day, was not so lucky. Sixty-three years old at the time of the trial, she stood accused of having cast a spell over a man named William Fynee, who had passed away the previous year after a short, unexpected illness. Agnes confessed to her role in his death and said that she had used magic to accomplish this. She said that she had asked the white cat to carry out her wishes, which included destroying the man's cattle and geese. After a falling out with another local woman, named Widow Gooday, Agnes is again said to have used her powers on a neighbor's livestock, asking the cat to drown the woman's cow. Similar spells were used to curdle milk and lose butter curds after Agnes was denied a request to share in some of her neighbor's food.

One big change from the work of Elizabeth is in the makeup of the familiar. While Satan had come to Agnes in the form of a big white cat, she had transformed him into a toad. Still the same being, the creature was now inhabiting a different body. Though she denied sharing her blood with the familiar, the courts took it upon themselves to examine Agnes's body and found a number of small pinpricks that they took as damning evidence. As well as this, she incorporated her daughter into her misdeeds. One day, she sent Joan to the home of the Brown family to ask for cheese and bread. Agnes Brown appeared at the door and turned down Joan's request. Joan, annoyed by the response, recalled what her mother did when annoyed and began to call upon the cat named Satan to avenge her. Suddenly, a black dog appeared before Joan and asked what she wanted. Afraid, Joan asked the creature to make young Agnes Brown feel similarly terrified. In response, the black dog asked for both her body and her soul.

Appearing in the court, Agnes Brown (a twelve-year-old) told the authorities of how that very same day a large black dog had appeared before her. Its face, she recalled, was similar to that of an ape and asked her for butter. Agnes Brown again denied the request, and so the dog went into the nearby cheese house without permission and settled a small silver whistle key upon the fresh produce. After the animal had vanished, the little girl ran to tell her mother, who in turn fetched a priest. The family was told to pray on the matter. The next day, the dog reappeared to the girl, again with the same key. When Agnes asked what it wanted, it mumbled "evil words" before leaving. The dog reappeared a third time, unexpectedly. This time, it came to the girl holding a knife in its mouth. It asked the little girl whether she was dead. The girl replied that she was not dead, then broke down into a desperate prayer. The dog informed her – according to the testimony given to the court - that if she would not die, the knife would be thrust into her chest. Calling on Jesus to drive the creature away, Agnes Brown asked who had sent him. The dog motioned towards the Waterhouse's home. When asked to show the dog in front of the court, Agnes Waterhouse admitted that she had no control over the beast.

While Joan, eighteen at the time, was eventually found not guilty, her mother was sentenced to death. Before she was hanged, Agnes Waterhouse made one final confession, in which she admitted to being a witch and carrying out "abominable deeds." She repented and asked for the forgiveness of God. She even confessed to having sent the cat named Satan one last time to kill a neighbor and damage his foods, but the cat returned to her saying that it would be impossible, suggesting that the intended target was too strong in the faith. Another of her confessions was that she always prayed in Latin, having been told to do so by the cat. This was a major strike against her in the eyes of the townsfolk, who decried her lack of English prayers. She was executed two days after the close of the trial, hanged on the 29th of July, 1566.

The case of the Chelmsford witches seems to demonstrate how women might confess – away from the threat of torture – to being involved in a conspiratorial plot. The witchcraft they admitted to undertaking was powerful and was believed to be legitimate by the rest of their community. As a landmark case in English law, it showed how the people of the time truly believed in the magic and the possibility that a person might invoke the spirit of the devil to do mischief. The notes of the trial teach us how this might have been done, using blood mixed with milk, offered up to a witch's familiar. While Elizabeth Francis managed to escape capital punishment, she was eventually condemned on a similar charge many years later. The reputation for magic, it seems, followed an individual for a long time.

Agnes's spell

Even though Agnes Waterhouse was executed for her meddling in the dark arts, some of the magic in her story is not dissimilar to that used by modern witches. In particular, the idea of a familiar is something that has never truly left the witching world. Rather than each witch trying to summon a representation of Satan himself, however, most magical practitioners find themselves better able to accomplish their goals once they have struck up a bond with a familiar. For most, these are regular household animals, the bond with whom is stronger than it would be with a typical pet. More on the level of a close friend or personal associate, the familiar provides a secure spiritual foundation on which the magic user can conduct their arts. In this particular spell, we will look into the process of fashioning a cat into a witch's familiar.

For this spell, you will need a number of items. First among these is, quite obviously, a cat. This should only ever be your own pet. It helps (especially for a beginner) to use an animal with which you already have a strong emotional bond. The bond must be reciprocated, i.e. a cat who you have known for some time and who is able to recognize and respond to your presence. For most people, this will be their own household cat. As well as the animal to be turned into a familiar, you will also need a set of pencils of various color, specifically those of your cat, one white candle, and a piece of blank paper.

First, you should wait until the first day of the month. Once it arrives, you will need to spend the morning drawing your cat to the best of your abilities. Use the colors to represent the exact features of your pet, though do not be worried about artistic skill. More important is the ability to try and represent the cat as you know it to be. This is why it is so important to work with an animal you already know. If the cat has any certain mannerisms or habits, then think about these during the sketching. If he had any distinctive marks, make sure they are represented. All the while, you should be thinking about the cat, keeping it in your mind's eye. Once it is complete, you should wait for noon and fold the piece of paper in two.

Take the piece of folded paper and write on one side the existing name of your cat. On the reverse of the folded sheet, you should write the name of your new familiar. The new name is the magical title it will have. This will be known only to you. Anything will work, but if one particular name keeps making itself clear to you, then this is likely for a reason. The only restriction is that it should be an entirely new name. Once both names are in place, take the candle and use it to draw a wax pentagram over each of the two names. After this is done, take the folded paper and place it beneath your pillow.

This is where the paper must remain for a month. As you sleep, the bond with your familiar will grow ever stronger. On the first day of the new month, take out the paper and burn it over the flame of the candle. Once it is nothing but ashes, the spell will be complete. Over the coming weeks, you should feel as though the bond between the two of you is growing increasingly stronger. After another month, the spell should be complete, and you will finally have your own familiar.

Malin Matsdotter

Throughout all of the turmoil and persecution that witches have faced during the length of human existence, there have been times when the fervor for their punishment has been at its highest. Occasionally, countries will recognize that they have become obsessed with the witch trials and will back off slightly. In Sweden, one of the original homes of European paganism, this occurred at the end of the seventeenth century. However, that is not before the next entry in the book, Malin Matsdotter, was prosecuted for the crime of being a witch. The last official victim of the huge Swedish witch hunt known as "the Great Noise," her story is a fascinating insight into witchcraft in a society that was beginning to realize how extreme they had taken their persecution of those thought to be interested in magic.

Like many of the women in this book, Malin was not a young woman. Having descended from Finnish ancestors, she had been living in the town of Mariberget, near Stockholm. By the year 1676, a huge country-wide hunt for witches had been taking place throughout Sweden, the scale of which was so massive that it was known as "the Great Noise." Typically, those who were found guilty of witchcraft during this time were decapitated and then burned, with many people living in fear of who might be the next person to be accused of magical practice. During the time, almost 300 people (both men and women) were accused of witchcraft and as a result, executed. The fervor reached its peak in 1675, when the trials arrived in a nearby town named Torsaker. Unlike many witch trials from across Europe, however, the chief accusation levelled against witches in Sweden was not necessarily that they were involved in dark magic, but rather that they were stealing children and taking them to black Sabbaths and offering them up to Satan. By the time the authorities reached Malin, they had already convicted and killed five other local women.

As we have mentioned, Malin Matsdotter was a poor old woman. Not well off, she was already a widow when she was accused, her husband having been tried, convicted, and executed by the local authorities for the crime of sodomy. It is not known what she did for money, though some scholars suspect that her skills as a midwife were highly valued in the community. A typical trade for those accused of witchcraft, the process of delivering a baby can be difficult, complicated, and bewildering enough to most as to appear as though it requires magic. Strangely enough, it was not the other townsfolk who accused Malin of stealing children, but rather her own daughters. Her offspring came forward to the authorities conducting the witch hunt in the area and put forward Malin's name, suggesting that the old woman had in fact stolen away their children and taken them to a devil worshiping even in the nearby Blockula. The accusations were enough to prompt Malin's arrest, and she was dragged from her home, cursing her daughters with every breath.

Placed in front of the court and told to answer for her sins, the old woman stood defiant. She refused to entertain the notion that she had stolen any children or was in any way a witch. But this adamant belief was taken by the court as simply more evidence. In their opinion, the only way this woman could be so forceful in her convictions was if she had been imbued with extra power by the devil himself.

After refusing to plead guilty to her crimes, and with her continued denial only convincing the judges of her guilt, Malin was sentenced to be executed. She had been tortured for extended periods of time, subjected to prolonged periods of pain and suffering in order to try and get her to confess. Still she refused. One of the women previously accused of witchcraft, Anna Larka, had found that her steadfast refusal to admit to her sins had also led to a death sentence, a judgement that was altered when she finally did confess. Unlike Larka, however, Malin was utterly adamant as to her own innocence. In light of this particularly iron will, the authorities decided that the normal method of execution was not enough. Rather than beheading the witch before placing her on the flames, Malin was sentenced to be burned alive.

This method of execution caused some consternation among the authorities. While they seemed happy enough to behead witches, burning them alive seemed a step too far. There emerged a schism among the judges, over whether the idea of "public burning" entailed that the victim need be alive when the punishment was carried out. Controversy raged while Malin, still protesting her innocence, waited to be lashed to the stake. At no other point in Swedish history was a person sentenced to be burned alive for the practice of witchcraft. This was to make Malin's case truly unique. Added to this, rarely was someone put to death when no confession had been put forward. As a compromise, some suggested that the accused might be given a chance to confess just before the burning. Should she admit to her crimes, then the execution would continue as normal, with the beheading before the flames. Another person put forward the idea that Mali might be tortured with hot irons in the hours leading up to her death, so much so that she would pass out from the pain and not be conscious when the fire was lit. All of these were rejected by the priest, who determined that the name of God must be held higher than the possibility of pain experienced by just one woman. As one concession, the authorities permitted Malin to hang a small bag of gun powder around her neck. As the flames got hotter and hotter, she would experience a great deal of pain, right up until the gunpowder exploded and destroyed her throat and chest. This, it seemed, was their method of providing a more humane death.

On the 5th of August, 1676, Malin was brought forward into the square in Hotorget, a district in Stockholm. Alongside her was another woman, Anna Simonsdotter, who had been similarly accused by her daughters of stealing away their children. Anna was to be given the standard method of execution and was beheaded. With such a marked difference between the two ensuing deaths, the reaction of Malin Matsdotter has been written into the history books. It was recorded that Anna stepped forward to be beheaded "with great humility." She seemed to respect the decision of the court and was said to have exhibited remorse, reading aloud extracts of psalms before falling to her knees and thrusting her face up to the heavens. She confessed to her crimes and begged for forgiveness from God. This was markedly different from Malin.

Unlike the other condemned woman, Malin remained firm and proud. She smiled as an attendant fixed the bag of gunpowder around her neck and fearlessly climbed up the stake. As she did so, she talked calmly to the executioners, thrusting her hands forward to be clasped in iron manacles. At no point did she fight or struggle. As she was prepared to be burned, Malin struck up a conversation with the attending priests. Holding her head high, she refused to acknowledge their pleas for her to confess. Even as she was being fastened to the stake, she shouted her innocence for everyone to hear. One of her daughters stepped forward from the crowd and demanded that her mother admit her guilt. Malin ignored the girl's questions, instead condemning the daughter to hell and cursing her soul for the rest of eternity. As the last words fell from her lips, the fire was set just below her feet.

By all accounts from the square in Stockholm, Malin Matsdotter seemed to be in no pain while she burned. For some, this was only further proof of her guilt. For others, it was a sign from God that they had executed the wrong woman and that heavenly powers had saved her from suffering. Predominantly, however, it only seemed to confirm the notion that witches felt no pain, though the entire event was traumatic for many authority figures. It was not long after this that the witch trials were abandoned in Sweden. Malin was the last person executed for such crimes. Instead, it began to become more and more regular for people to start doubting those who came forward to accuse people of witchcraft. Of the other people accused of witchcraft and awaiting execution, all were set free, while those witnesses who were now believed to have made up their stories were executed in their stead, one of whom was Malin's daughter. Other witnesses, their crimes not deemed to have been as great, were simply whipped. In 1677, an order was sent out that compelled all of the priests in the country to tell their congregations that every witch in Sweden had been expelled. With that, the Great Noise came to an end. Aside from scattered examples and accusations, the enthusiasm of the trials was never again seen in the country.

The story of Malin Matsdotter might not tell us much about the specific characteristics of witchcraft, but it can show us how the constant accusations and executions eventually took a toll on a society. After one particularly brutal execution, the rest of the country quickly came to terms with the idea that the witchcraft they were constantly chasing might not be entirely true. From this point in history, witches were freer to practice their art. While still keeping quiet about their beliefs, it was recognized that old women with skills and ancient knowledge might not necessarily be in league with the devil. While most refused to trust witches and those who practiced magic, there was at least an end to the large scale executions and slaughter of anyone with more than a passing interest in the occult.

Malin's spell

For anyone wondering whether Malin Matsdotter actually possessed magical interests, the records passed down from the Swedish courts do not tell us much. Due in part to her steadfast refusal to admit to being involved in any form of witchcraft, least of all the crimes of which she was accused, we can only guess as to the kind of spells she might have used. As such, with the story of her calmly going to her death, we can speculate on the possibility that she might have used a protective charm. Common enough among magical users, protection spells can be entrusted with guarding you against physical and emotional pain. While it might take a very powerful witch indeed to protect against raging flames, a beginner can try their luck with this simple spell designed to offer protection over the coming days. This spell will take a month to put together, so do not expect instant results.

This is an incredibly easy spell and needs very little in the way of tools. All you will require is a small vial in which you can keep water. Once you have this, the first step is to fill it up. Don't worry about where your water comes from – tap water will suffice in this case. What matters is what we will do to it and what the water will become. With the vial filled with water, you must wait until the beginning of a new moon. Now, take the vial and place it on the window sill nearest to where you sleep. Before you go to bed every night, cup the vial between your hands and think about every positive thing that has happened to you during the day. Concentrate very hard, spending a few minutes doing this every night. Do so for a month, pouring your positive emotions into the vial and the water within. There are no magic words, just the transfer of energies and the moonlight.

Once a lunar month has passed and the moon is new once again, your preparation work will be complete. Now, every morning before you leave the house, you should sprinkle some of the water on to your wrists. A light protection spell, this can help guard you against those small annoyances and micro-aggressions that we encounter every day. Depending on the size of the vial, you may wish to have a system in which you are setting up one vial as you are using another. This way, you will always have access to your protective water.

Mother Shipton

Not every witch in this book has been accused of terrible crimes. In some instances, the witches we will look at have been exalted for their incredible powers and hailed as truly magical people. While we might have a tainted historical view of witchcraft that is replete with accusations and negative perceptions, some people have come to be revered for their ability to turn the magical arts to their will. One such person is known simply as Mother Shipton.

Born by the name Ursula Southeil, Mother Shipton lived during a time in which the belief in witchcraft was rampant. Slightly before the main threat of the witch trials, her magic was instead focused on a very different practice: divination. Known as a soothsayer and a prophetess, her ability to predict the future was well known throughout her native England and meant that she was something of a celebrity, despite her magical leanings. While other women might have been condemned for their witchcraft, Mother Shipton's fame lived on long after her death. In fact, the majority of her predictions were not published until long after she had died. Not one to predict the end of the world like so many other supposed prophets would have people believe, her predictions were often a lot more local. But who exactly was she and what did she predict?

Most of the information that we have about Mother Shipton comes from the books she wrote. While she was a legend in her own lifetime, much of the contemporary information is marred by mistruths, exaggerations, and typical mythology. However, we can piece together some facts.

She was born in Yorkshire, in the north of England. There is a cave in Knaresborough which, to this day, is regarded as the site of her birth and which now bears her name. We believe that she was likely a very ugly woman, marked by some sort of disfigurement that caused great concern to those who looked upon her face. As is claimed in the book, in 1512 she may well have married a man named Tom Shipton, who ran a local carpentry business. That is essentially all of the information that we can glean from her literary legacy, though there is one interesting cross reference that it can be interesting to note. The famed diarist Samuel Pepys, writing in the 17th Century, recorded a conversation happening at the Royal Court regarding the predictions that the prophetess Mother Shipton had made. Thanks to this extant reference, we can gather than her fame had at least spread as far south as London during the years after her death.

For many people, Mother Shipton's predictions are best known through a certain edition of her book. Written in verse, the book is in fact an amalgamation of many of the earlier works we have attributed to the soothsayer. It takes the information and reshapes it. Though many people misguidedly accept this as the correct version, it is in fact far from the real thing. This version was in fact published in 1862 and includes many predictions that were invented by the author or which cannot be sourced. The man who we suspect of this forgery, Charles Hindely, seemed to admit as much many years later, by which time the damage was done. Because of this, many people doubt the veracity of many of the more authentic predictions, due to the fact that they have been mixed in with the newer, false inventions.

Instead, many scholars have worked to separate the original predictions from the ideas that were invented by Hindley and others who had hoped to capitalise on the legend of the witch. Some of these (now famous) predictions were held to be incredibly accurate and true. This was because they had been written after the events and secretly inserted into the texts. For example, entries invented by Hindley seemed to suggest that the old Yorkshire woman had predicted everything from the existence of submarines, to the construction of Crystal Palace, to the Crimean War, as well as the discovery of tobacco and the potato. But the most notorious predictions attributed to Mother Shipton during the 19th Century were often simply false. We must cast aside these predictions and note them for what they really are: inventions that were placed into the tome after the witch's death.

Thanks to the meddling of these people trying to interfere with the legacy of one of Britain's most famous witches, we may never know which of the prophecies are truly hers (and were accurate) and which were inserted after the fact. We might be able to assume that those that seem almost too accurate to be true were likely constructed in the name of selling more and more books. However, there are certain entries that are markedly different from the rest. In these predictions, Mother Shipton does not seem to try and predict the outcome of world wars and far flung inventions. Instead, her ideas are much more local. Those who have studied Knaresborough and Yorkshire during the time when she lived have discovered that prophecies relating to such events as great storms, poor harvests, and bouts of illness can be read into the old woman's work. These passages are usually ignored by the more modern reader, simply as they appear as though they are filler between the more interesting, flashier predictions. However, in the view of many, these entries are in fact the skeletal remains of the real predictions made by the witch in Yorkshire. Thanks to the studies that have been commissioned and investigations conducted into the history of one of the country's most famous witches, it slowly becomes possible to untangle the more likely predictions from those that were simply inserted to make money from gullible readers.

In her time, Mother Shipton was a recluse. She was a hermit who lived alone in a cave and offered up her apparently prophetic knowledge to the locals who were scared to look at her. She had a reputation as a witch, an ugly old woman who strolled hastily along the line of sanity. But in her ability to predict the things of local importance (weather, crops, sickness), she was a valuable resource. As such, this is likely where her story gained so much initial traction. Thanks to the fervent belief in her ability to predict phenomena in a genuinely useful manner, the locals put aside their typical fear of witches and instead turned to Mother Shipton as a font of knowledge.

Perhaps this is why her case is so different from many example of witchcraft that we read about in this book. While many of the more threatening witches were treated in a horrible manner and often tortured or killed, this particular witch was demonstrably useful to the local population. As such, she built up a reputation and legend that was handed down from generation to generation. She was tolerated for her usefulness, rather than feared for her "otherness." When examining the history of some of the most powerful witches ever to have lived, the story of Mother Shipton stands out in the way in which she was treated by her contemporaries. Rather than being hounded out of the village or tied to a burning stake, she was instead treated with respect. Even if she was likely not loved by the local population, she at least provided an example to medieval peoples of how – when used benevolently – witches and magic might be of use. In this respect, the truth behind her predictions is almost irrelevant. While most women were executed on even the slightest hint they might be a witch, the usefulness of Mother Shipton meant that she instead became a local legend in a town where her cave dwelling is still a popular tourist spot to this day.

Mother Shipton's spell

Anyone who reads the story of Mother Shipton will no doubt start wondering just how they might be able to use their own magical abilities to make predictions about the future. For many witches, these kind of prophecies appear as a weak intuition, a sensation, or a feeling that something make happen. Almost like a magical kind of instinct, they can become more and more refined as we grow older. However, there are ways in which we can use tools and equipment in order to throw these thoughts into greater focus. One such tool is named a scrying mirror. These mirrors are ancient, wonderful devices that can be perfect for those who believe they possess some kind of second sight and would like some help with making their visions clearer.

Despite the name, a scrying mirror is not your typical household mirror. Instead, it is colored a deep black. Rather than looking at reflections or yourself, you are supposed to be looking deep into the abyss, staring as hard as possible into the blackest depths in order to make sense of and clarify your thoughts. As such, the tools that you will need are simple. First, you will need a piece of clear glass. This can be a glass plate, the glass from a photo frame, or even a piece of a smashed window. It must be transparent, and it must not be too big. A dinner plate is usually the perfect size for beginners, though more advanced users often favor something smaller. As well as this, you will need paints. The most important is a matte black paint that will adhere to your glass object. Try and get the deepest, densest black possible. In addition, some people wish to make adornments and additions, so an alternative color paint can be used for decoration. This is optional, however.

To create your scrying mirror, simply apply the thick black paint to the rear of the glass. You should have an idea which side you will be using to peer into, so be sure to paint the other side. Don't worry too much about brush strokes. Ideally, there will be small marks, patterns, and lines that will be useful in the near future. What is important is that you cover the material completely and are able to ensure that no light can pierce through the black paint. Once it is completely covered, then you will need to leave it to dry. If you feel like decorating the mirror (perhaps with pentagrams or inscriptions), wait until the black paint is dry and then feel free to continue. Doing so will only make the mirror feel as though it is more personalized, so it will not harm the tool's effectiveness.

Once the paint is dry and you have added any decorative marks you wish, then it is time to ensure that the mirror has the correct energies. This is a simple process and requires only a very old tree and moonlight. You should venture out and attempt to find the oldest tree you possibly can. It should be as old as possible, but the species does not matter. What matters are the correct energies and the connection with the earth. Once you have found the right tree, you should wait for the day before a full moon. Bury the mirror at the foot of the tree and leave it there for three days. Once you return (after the full moon has passed), then you should uncover the mirror and take it home with you. You have now created your very own scrying mirror.

This might be all well and good, but how should you use such an object? The truth is that there is no simple way to get good at these kinds of divination spells. There is only practice. Scrying works best when it is in tune with your own intuitions, so you should wait until you have the sensations coursing through your body. Occasionally you might be struck by an energy or an idea that seems as though it is hinting at more to come. When this happens, go to your mirror. Take it out and lay it on a flat surface. Now, peer deeply into the darkness of the black surface. Beneath the glass, you should see the brush strokes and the tiny marks that are present in any such device. Putting aside your thoughts for a second, begin to focus on these tiny irregularities. Watch then weave in and out of one another, allowing your mind to delve deeper and deeper into the darkness. When you are suitably relaxed, slowly bring forward those same energies that first inspired you. Keep tracing the shapes and patters in the plate, while allowing your vision to make itself clearer. It is a difficult process, but you will gradually learn how to entertain fully formed visions in your head. While you might struggle at first, there is only one way to get better. Practice. Whenever you feel the urge, venture to your scrying mirror. One day, you might be able to see the truth of the world just like Mother Shipton.

Joan Wytte

These days, the world's views on witches are largely very different from days of yore. Whereas once they were feared and chased across the country, there is now a genuine curiosity and interest in the skills and abilities that they possess. Accordingly, there is now an effort to look throughout history and examine the way in which many of the people accused of witchcraft were treated. While there is nothing that can be done to help these long-dead witches, there are examples of the modern person attempting to do right by their ancestors. As interest in witchcraft, Wicca, paganism, and other types of magic grows and grows, we will perhaps find more cases like that of Joan Wytte.

Joan Wytte's story is typical of many people thought to have been witches at one time or another. A woman from Bodmin, in Cornwall, she earned a reputation for fighting fairies. Indeed, her nickname was the Fairy Fighting Woman of Bodmin, a name that more than hints at the magical backdrop to her life. Having been born in 1775, she was alive after the majority of the European witch trials had come to a close. She was not old when she died, just 38, and spent her last days with bronchial pneumonia, cooped up inside the local jail. From a family of weavers, she was the victim of the industry falling on hard times and the family finding themselves without much money. Instead, local records list her profession as a "tawner," one who made white leather. The process was difficult and often involved treating cow hides to some of the most horrible substances around. This would usually meant that few people wanted to socialize with a tawner, and the trade was left to the social outcasts. Bodmin, however, was at least partly known for their high quality white leather, which would be used to make gloves, shoes, and boots for the richer members of society.

At the time, she had a reputation as a clairvoyant. She was known to possess "second sight," to be a naturally gifted interpreter of the signs and signals that are passed down through the spirits. One of her most famous tricks involves items known as "clooties," which were thin strips of cloth to be taken from a person who was ill. These strips of cloth were tied to a tree. The belief was a form of sympathetic magic, in that the cloth would bind the energies and negative emotions of the patient, and while the cloth rotted around the tree, would soon help to dispel these evils. This was a service Joan would perform for the people in the local town, though as she aged, she found herself with fewer and fewer customers. Her demeanor is often cited as the cause. We know that she was an irascible woman, not prone to conversing lightly with anyone and getting angry at the drop of a hat.

Some have blamed this on a possible tooth abscess that she may have contracted and had no means to treat. Getting into a lot of fights, she exhibited prodigious fighting abilities, something that some people blamed on her being in league with the devil. She was imprisoned for fighting when she passed away, locked up in the local jail, a place cold and wet enough to inevitably lead to her demise. Her skeleton was kept, used as a sort of exhibition for the locals. But the reputation of the Fighting Fairy Woman lived on in local legend.

Apart from these biographical details, the rest of our information about Joan's life arrives after her death. For many years, her skeleton could be found hanging in the Museum of Witchcraft found in Boscastle. A Cornish museum dedicated to all types of the occult in the area, the bones were hung in front of a coffin as part of an exhibit. Joan was a small woman whose reputation for fighting fairies was partly born out of her aggressive nature and a string of vicious assaults. When a new curator took over the museum in the late 1990s, he noted that many of the children visiting the museum would be scared by the skeleton, treating it with fear and scorn simply because it belonged to a seemingly monstrous witch. After some paranormal and strange disturbances in the museum during the night, a consultant was brought in. The consultant immediately noticed that the lack of a fitting and respectful burial might be what was causing the witch's spirit to linger long after her death. She was reburied in a secret spot, away from the prying eyes of the public and known only to a few select people.

However, before the body was laid to rest, scientists were given the chance to take a forensic look at the skeleton of the woman believed to be a witch. Thanks to the rigorous experiments conducted on the woman's remains, they were able to shed some extra light on the life of a witch hundreds of years ago, the kind of raw data that is rarely available to those with an interest in the realm of witchcraft. As expected, the first things the government inspectors found was that the skeleton belonged to a woman aged around 38 years old, exactly as the records said. But they also deduced that she was a regular smoker of tobacco and favored a clay pipe when she indulged. A large portion of her diet, it seemed, consisted of stone ground flour. This perhaps led to the short stature, which could have been the result of continued under-nourishment over the course of her life. Looking closely at her build, they found that Joan possessed long arms and a very slim figure, with fingers that were almost like the claws of birds in their spindly nature.

While there was little evidence of conditions such as arthritis, there was certainly enough to point the scientists towards two interesting assumptions. One of these is that we can look deep into what could be found in the Wytte home. High in fluoride, the entire family likely drank from the same source at all times. Similarly, the bones showed scientists that their owners had spent a lot of time in contact with china clay, otherwise known as kaolin. The substance can be found close to Bodmin and gives us an insight into the whereabouts of Joan's home, especially when cross-referenced with the fluoride information. What's more, the scientists were able to examine the teeth inside the skull of the deceased witch and found that there was a huge cavity lurking beneath one of the woman's untreated wisdom teeth. This would have caused the owner a huge amount of pain and can likely account for Joan's notorious attitude and penchant for fighting.

Over the years, the skeleton was occasionally pillaged for souvenirs. Those with an interest in the occult were thought to be responsible for the stealing of several small finger bones and chipping away at other parts of the skeleton. As legend would have it, these artefacts were then used in dark magic ceremonies, in which séances and gatherings looked to the bones of the dead witch in order to guide them through their own attempts at replicating some of her arts. But as it stands, there are no reports of any of these gathering resulting in success. Rather than eliciting the dead witch's spirit, they seem only to have angered her further. Now finally taken away from the abscess in her mouth that likely caused so much pain, the spirit of the dead woman likely did not want to return to the land of the living. This is part of the reason why the owner of the skeleton decided to lay Joan in an unmarked grave. Whether it was people who were still scared of the witch's power or those who were fascinated by what she represented, he believed that there would be no rest for the bones while people still knew their location. In a small gathering and a private ceremony, the remains of Joan Wytte were laid to rest once and for all.

The treatment of these bones in modern times tells us a great deal about the changing attitudes towards witchcraft over the ages. Combining the investigations into the bones by the Home Office and the local legends that endure to this day, we now have a fairly complete idea of who Joan Wytte was as a person. Thanks to the complete picture, we can gather together the image of a woman, blinded by pain, who nevertheless wanted to do some good in society. Her attempts at witchcraft were her passing on ancient knowledge and trying to heal those around her in a way that she could not do for herself. Without the privileges of modern dentistry, there was little that could be done about her pain. But as she grew worse and angrier, people started to shun the woman. Instead of attacking and killing the witch, those in the 18th Century seemed more tolerable to the ideas she possessed. Perhaps because she had spent so long helping the locals, she was never chased from town. Furthermore, in the modern age, enough respect for her craft and her memory exists that she received a proper burial. As attitudes toward witches have changed over the course of time, we have seen the change from those burned at the stake, to those ostracized, to those who are now respected enough to be finally, privately laid to rest. In that respect, the case of the Fairy Fighting Woman of Bodmin is an important milestone in society's attitudes towards magical practitioners.

Joan's spell

As we have already mentioned, the spell most commonly associated with Joan is the "clooties." These magical items are part of Cornish folklore but have been used elsewhere around the world for centuries. It's likely that Joan learned the ancient knowledge as it was passed down from generation to generation. While it might not be successful as a replacement for some of the most capable aspects of modern medicine, it can be used as a mild form of pain relief, especially among true believers. Instead of carrying out the practice on yourself, it is usually better as a means of relieving pain for other people. For beginners, it can be tried out when a friend or associate is experiencing something like a common cold. As you get better, you may wish to try with more debilitating illnesses. But, as is always important to note, those with actual medical conditions should always consult a doctor first and foremost.

If you do decide to use clooties, then you should be pleased to learn that there is very little that you actually need to bring to the table to carry out this particular spell. However, it can be difficult to find the right resources. Namely, a tree old and secure enough to take the illness and clothes that the patient is willing to be ripped in order to carry out the magic. For the first one, it can help to wander through a local park or woodland. You will be looking for a tree that has grown up over a long time. As the lifespan for trees can go one for hundreds of years, those who are able to find a truly old specimen will be those who are able to find one that has already seen great illness during its lifetime. That it has survived so far demonstrates its resilience and its ability to cope with the worst suffering imaginable. Once you have found yourself the right tree, then you should remember it. It is possible to use the same one over and over again, though be careful not to place too much of a burden on the plant.

Once you have the right tree in mind, then you will need to be able to rip strips from the patient's clothes. Typically, most people are not happy with the idea of their favorite items being torn up, so it can help to use a piece of clothing intended to be ripped. All that matters is that the item has spent some time being worn by the person, especially during their sickness. Purchasing a cheap t-shirt and having the patient wear it for a short time is an excellent way around this. Once you have found the right item of clothing, you will need to approach the patient and remove the strips while they are still wearing the clothes. While you can use scissors, it is usually better is you are able to rip the material by hand. You need a strip an inch wide and as long as possible. Sometimes, a small incision with scissors or a knife can help, then the hands can be used to rip away the remaining material. Once you have the strips or clooties in hand, then you are free to move on to the next step.

Now, you must leave your patient behind. You must go back to the tree you found earlier and take the strips of material with you. You will fix the clooties to the tree, wrapping them around branches and tying them in a knot. Tie it tightly so that they will not move and fall away. Once you have attached the clooties to the tree, then you simply leave them. The energies that passed from the patient into the material will now pass once again into the tree. From here, it will be disseminated into the air and soil, diluted until the illness can no longer cause any damage. As the material soaks into the wood and eventually rots away, you should discover the patient recovering. In these days of modern medicine, there are often faster acting ways of dealing with the issue available from your doctor. But for those looking for a traditional, natural cure for their illness, the clooties can provide a great healing remedy.

Rosaleen "Roie" Norton

The last entry into this book is certainly more modern. While we have looked at witches from millennia ago, we can now examine how witches might function in the kind of society with which we are more familiar. Rosaleen

Norton is a fantastic example of this, taking the positon as one of the quintessential examples of a self-proclaimed, 20th Century witch.

Just as we look at the modern concept of a witch, it should perhaps be appropriate that we look to a country that has little history in the way of witch trials, Australia. Rosaleen Norton was born just east of Australia, in Dunedin, New Zealand. According to the stories she told, she was born during a thunderstorm and arrived at half past four in the morning on the 2nd of October, 1917. Her family was English and Christian, having recently moved to the country with their young daughters. Rosaleen's sisters were both over ten years older than her, but that wouldn't matter to the woman who claimed to have been born a witch. For evidence, she points towards her pointed ears, the blue-colored marks found on her knee, and a strand of dangling flesh that was hanging off her newborn body. When she was eight, the entire family moved across the ocean to live in Sydney, Australia.

As a child, Rosaleen knew she did not want to be like other children. She felt herself to be different. Always striving to be unconventional and not liking the other children, she found herself constantly coming into conflict with a variety of authority figures and, in particular, her mother. Thanks to his job as a sailor, her father was rarely at home. His wages allowed the family a comfortable life, though Rosaleen would not look back favorably on her childhood. She described it as "wearisome" and "detestable." Her constant striving for individuality even led to her refusing to sleep in the house, setting up a small tent in the garden instead.

Kept in the entrance to the tent was her pet spider, which she named Horatius, the first of a number of animals she formed attachments to over the years.

Rosaleen was sent off to a school run by the Church of England, though she did not last too long in such an institution. Eventually expelled for being too disruptive, she particularly perturbed the school authorities by her habit of drawing vampires and demons on every available surface. This, the teachers claimed, was corrupting the other pupils. Sent instead to a technical college, she found herself falling under the tutelage of a sculpting instructor named Rayner Hoff, who noted a burgeoning artistic talent in the girl. He encouraged Rosaleen to express herself via her art and in return, earned her respect.

After leaving school, Rosaleen had her mind set on becoming a professional writer. Some of her horror stories were published in a newspaper in 1934, when she was just sixteen. These stories led to the paper appointing her as a journalist and illustrator, though in a very minor position. When they got a look at her artwork, however, they were horrified. The images were deemed to be far too controversial and the young girl lost her job. Around the same time, the death of Rosaleen's mother led to her moving out of the family home. She found work posing for artists in Sydney, as well as working as a maid in a hospital, waitressing, and even designing toys. Taking a room above an old bar, she found her interests piqued when reading through ancient books on demonology, the occult, and other alternative religions.

Beresford Conroy met Rosaleen Norton in 1935. They were married in 1940. For their honeymoon, the pair went hitchhiking across the country, travelling through some of the biggest cities in Australia. By the time they finally returned to Sydney, Beresford felt compelled to enlist in the army and was shipped off to fight in the Second World War. By the time he came back, he realized that he did not love his wife any more. Rosaleen had been struggling while her husband had been away, at one point reduced to sleeping in a stable. Beresford told her that he wanted a divorce, and the matter was finally settled in 1951. Taking up a room in a boarding house, Rosaleen found herself exposed to the more progressive sections of the local cultural movements. One magazine employed her as an illustrator, publishing her artworks at a time when they were increasingly influenced by her reading paganism. The more she drew and the more she researched the topics, the more Rosaleen found herself increasingly drawn to witchcraft.

While working for the magazine called Pertinent, Rosaleen encountered one of the most influential figures in her life. She met an artist named Gavin Greenless, whose surrealist art and poetry clicked with the young girl. The two were soon close friends, and they too went hitchhiking across Australia. They wanted to find a venue where Rosaleen might finally be able to put on an exhibition of her more challenging art. They finally found a place, owned by the University of Melbourne, where they showed 46 paintings. The exhibition proved hugely controversial. It lasted just two days, after which the police arrived and confiscated four of the more provocative works, whose subjects included witches and the devil. Charged with being obscene, Rosaleen was dragged into court. Though she managed to win the case (and was awarded a small settlement), she had already built up a reputation as a controversial figure.

Now notorious, Rosaleen moved back to Sydney, taking a room in the city's red light district. Quite well known in the local community, she was now able to find a receptive group for her challenging art pieces. Decorating her home in an occult manner, she found herself at the center of many people's attentions. The police were constantly seeking ways in which they might shut down her witchcraft-orientated lifestyle, but the search proved fruitless. A book of her work was published in 1952, including works with titles such as Black Magic and The Rites of Baron Samedi. Just 500 copies were published, but it was enough to stir the ire of many of the more conservative thinkers in the country. With two of the works ruled as obscene by a judge, existing copies of the book had to be edited to remove the pictures in question. In the United States, a similar controversy resulted in copies of the book being destroyed. Despite the large amount of publicity generated, and the fact that Rosaleen Norton's name was now famous, the affair bankrupted the publisher.

Anna Karina Hoffman, a vagrant who suffered from poor mental health, was detained in 1955 for swearing at a police officer. During her trial, she claimed to have been part of a black mass organized by Rosaleen Norton. This was vehemently denied by Rosaleen, who thought herself more of a pagan witch than a Satanist. The charges were later dropped after Hoffman admitted she had lied, but by that point, Rosaleen had already acquired a reputation in the press as a Satan worshipping witch. The stories they printed included the claim that she had been involved in animal sacrifices, something that Rosaleen not only denied, but also found to be horrific. Regardless of the truth behind the claims, they were enough to rile up police interest and cause them to look closely at Rosaleen's life.

One famous event involved the famed British composer, Sir Eugene Goossens. After Rosaleen's reputation reached the musician, he reached out to her, and the pair become close friends and then lovers. At one point, Goossens was arrested when trying to bring sexually explicit materials into Australia and was later "sectioned"[1] due to his suffering from schizophrenia. Despite this debilitating condition, Rosaleen continued to visit and support her friend. This lasted until 1964, when he was temporarily released. However, Goossens had another breakdown and attempted to kill Rosaleen with a kitchen knife. He would be sent back to the asylum until long after Rosaleen had passed away.

As the fifties and sixties passed by, Rosaleen's fame grew. Wrongly or not, she was regarded as a Satanist, and this drew interest from all quarters. Witchcraft, still illegal at the time, was a controversial subject, though she had no qualms about announcing herself publically as a witch. Attempts were made in interviews to explain her beliefs, but few people wanted to listen to her. Instead, she made money thanks to her paintings and her ability to cast hexes and spells for people. By the

---

[1]. Being sectioned means being admitted to a hospital whether or not you agree to it. The legal authority for your admission to the hospital comes from a Country's own law on mental health, like the Mental Health Act in England, rather than from your consent. This is usually because you are unable or unwilling to consent

time she died of colon cancer in 1979, Rosaleen had grown more and more reclusive. Though she had done a huge amount to spread awareness and knowledge of witchcraft in Australia and beyond, many of her real beliefs were still misinterpreted by a mainstream audience. Since then, many of her paintings have been sold at auction, while her life has been the subject of plays, research, and television dramas. Following her death, her writing and ideas about neopagan witchcraft have greatly contributed to the canon and have been embraced by many others.

The story of Rosaleen Norton shows us just how different – and yet similar – the cultural idea of witchcraft has become over the years. Though she was not executed like so many of her forebears, she was nevertheless harassed by the authorities and had her beliefs willfully misinterpreted. There is still a countercultural element to the paganist witchcraft she practiced, but this has done a great deal to knock down the barriers in our society. Since her death and the rise of movements such as Wicca and Kabbalah, the interest in reviving ancient forms of witchcraft is steadily becoming more and more culturally acceptable. Soon we might reach the point where witchcraft ranks alongside every other mode of belief and is granted the same privileges. Until then, there will always be an outsider element to those who are hoping to learn the trade. For many, this is a large part of the appeal.

Rosaleen's spell

Rosaleen Norton was highly involved in creating what we now recognize as Neopaganism. As such, the final spell we look at is one of the spells used by the followers of her art form. This is a pagan spell designed to provide protection. To get it right, you will need the following: a small stone, a hammer, a single black feather, a strip of paper that you have torn, and a little black bag. You will notice that, unlike many of our previous spells, the items used to conduct this incantation are much closer to nature. That is due to paganism's (and Neopaganism's) close bonds with the living world. Once you have gathered everything together, then we will be ready to begin.

First, pick up the stone. It should be roughly the size of a coin and can be either coarse or smooth. Now, take the hammer and hit the stone just hard enough to break it in two. The pieces do not have to be exact, but a rough split between the two is best. Once you have the two pieces, plus any smaller ones that came apart, place them inside the bag. Take the feather, run it through the space between your fingers and then place that in the bag as well. Should the feather prove to be too long to fit (likely), then you can use a pair of scissors to cut it down to size. Simply put all the separated pieces into the bag. Roll the paper into a tight curl, and place that also into the bag.

Once everything is securely inside, you will need to tie the bag up tight. This is why many people use a drawstring bag, though it is possible to use anything else (such as string) to seal shut a standard black bag. Now, take the bag and bury it as close as possible to the front door of your home. If this is not possible, then you can place it near the door and pile items on top of it, essentially burying it on the inside. Once it is in a secure place, the energies from the bag will spread out and will cover the home in a protective spell. This will prevent against bad luck and could well bring some good fortune into your life.

Conclusion

Throughout this book, we have seen the ways in which witchcraft and witches have been treated over the centuries. From the earliest origins as part of Greek mythology to the counterculture movement that somehow got sidetracked into Satanism, there has been a consistent and sometimes damaging fascination with the magical world. Some of the people in this book were likely not witches, but that truth did not matter to those who thought them to be magical creatures regardless of the evidence that was placed before them.

The world of witchcraft and magic is a truly incredible place. Nowadays, we have entire communities dedicated to art forms that in the past would have gotten you killed. The spells we have included in this book might have been enough to condemn someone to death, had they been seen in public talking about such matters. As well as this, we have included a list of further reading materials that you might enjoy and that might let you further into the magical realm.

Whether you wish to become a witch or are just fascinated by magic in all its forms, witchcraft will always hold a special place in many people's hearts. As you travel further down the magical road, you might find yourself more and more enthralled by the possibilities offered by the ancient and wonderful knowledge.

Further Reading

Alexander, S., MacGregor, T., Singer, M. and Singer, M. (2012). *The only book of Wiccan spells you'll ever need*. Avon, Mass.: Adams Media.

Bell, T. (n.d.). *Wicca teachings*.

Beth, R. (1995). *The Wiccan path*. Freedom, CA: Crossing Press.

Beth, R. (2008). *Spellcraft for hedge witches*. London: Robert Hale.

Crowley, A. (1980). *The book of lies*. York Beach, Me.: S. Weiser.

Crowley, A. and Harris, F. (1974). *The book of Thoth*. York Beach, Me.: S. Weiser.

Crowley, V. (2003). *Wicca*. London: Element.

Cunningham, S. (1989). *Wicca*. St. Paul, Minn., U.S.A.: Llewellyn Publications.

Heselton, P. (2012). *Witchfather*. Loughborough, Leicestershire: Thoth Publications.

Higginbotham, J. and Higginbotham, R. (2002). *Paganism*. St. Paul, Minn.: Llewellyn Publications.

Jennings, P. (2002). *Pagan paths*. London: Rider.

Murphy-Hiscock, A. (2005). *Solitary Wicca for life*. Avon, Mass.: Provenance Press/Adams Media.

Pennick, N. (2001). *The pagan book of days*. Rochester, Vt.: Destiny Books.

Sabin, T. (2006). *Wicca for beginners*. Woodbury, Minn.: Llewellyn Publications.

West, K. (2005). *The real witches' craft*. London: Element.

Image Credits

The Three Witches from Shakespeares Macbeth by Daniel Gardner [Public domain], via Wikimedia Commons

Medea, Frederick Sandys, 1866-1868, Birmingham Museum and Art Gallery

Depiction of the Devil giving magic puppets to witches, from Agnes Sampson trial, 1591. Unknown.

An image of a witch and her familiar spirits taken from a publication that dealt with the witch trials of Elizabeth Stile, Mother Dutten, Mother Devell and Mother Margaret in Windsor, 1579. Late sixteenth century. Unknown.

1920 painting of Marie Laveau (1794–1881) by Frank Schneider, based on an 1835 painting (now lost?) by George Catlin.

Gedenkstätte zur Hexenverfolgung in Fulda

Woodcut of Agnes Waterhouse the first person to be executed as a witch in England. c1566

Häxprocess i Mora 1670. Tyskt kopparstick. I förgunden djävlar och häxor. Där ovan förhörskommissionen med en hop klagande kvinnor och barn som avger vittnesmål. En fångknekt driver fram en flock fängslade häxor och trollkarlar. Omkring bålet där de dömda brinner, syns häxor som bortför barn på sopkvastar, bockar och dynggrepar medan demoner i djurskepnad tumlar i luften.

Old engraving of Mother Shipton. Unknown date.

A Visit to the Witch. 1882. Edward Frederick Brewtnall.

A black and white photograph of witch and artist Rosaleen Norton. Printed in Nevill Drury's Homage to Pan. Rosaleen Norton

More Books by Desmond Wilde

Witchcraft and Magick have existed for thousands of years. Everyone can learn to practice Witchcraft and Magick. It is time to tap into your supernatural self and empower your life with the knowledge of witchcraft and magick.

This beginner's guide includes all the information you need to start your journey into the world of witchcraft to unleash your spirituality and help you discover your magickal powers.

Wicca holds a rich tradition of natural and supernatural solutions to the problems which people face. Sometimes referred to as magic, magick, witchcraft, or the occult, Wicca is just one branch of the kind of thinking which intrigues and fascinates so many people.

For those who are interested in entering the world of Wicca, this guide is designed to provide you with an armory of introductory spells which can be used by beginner practitioners right away.

Learn many of the ancient arts discovered by our mystical ancestors. While they once might have used them to form potions and love spells, we can now turn this knowledge toward being able to attract wealth and fortune towards your person. We will not be turning lead into gold, though. Instead, you will be able to prepare yourself spiritually for one of the most difficult and hard to enact branches of magick.

By learning the arts described in this book, you can place yourself into the perfect position for wealth to move toward you. Magick often moves in mysterious ways, and those who are looking for clearly defined answers are often in entirely the wrong place.

Printed in Great Britain
by Amazon